Where's Rick?

Where's Rick?

Ten Months after Returning Home, a Vietnam Vet Goes Missing

Buck Buchanan

Broadway Ventures, LLC
Marietta, Georgia

Where's Rick?

Buck Buchanan

Published by:
    Broadway Ventures, LLC
    192 Blair Valley Drive NE
    Marietta, GA 30060

Copyright © Broadway Ventures, LLC, 2023

ISBN: 979-8-218-18551-0
$16.99 U.S.

Cover Image: Cindy Buchanan

Table of Contents

Acknowledgements

I want to thank my wife Cindy, who designed the cover of this book and puts up with my writing career.

I also want to thank Retired Colonel Johnnie B. Hitt, who served in the U.S. Army as helicopter Aircraft Commander during the Vietnam War. He gave me some valuable information about the war and what it was like being assigned to an Assault Helicopter platoon.

Once again, many thanks to Deke Castleman, who edited my book. As always, he was great to work with.

Dedication

This book is dedicated to the men and women who served our country during the Vietnam conflict—those who gave their lives or survived the horrors of war and were forever changed.

Vietnam vets served just as other soldiers had in wars before and after, except when they returned home, things were different. Instead of being welcomed as heroes, many were greeted by rowdy mobs that spewed hatred.

The Vietnam soldiers had the most difficult job, because not only did they have to fight the enemy, but when they returned home, they also had to fight for respect. They regained that respect, but it took many years before our country embraced and recognized them. Today, we thank them for their service.

Author's Note

This is a work of non-fiction; all the details in this book are true. Most of the information comes from newspaper clippings as the events took place. The story unfolded between 1971 and 1975, primarily in Chattanooga, Tennessee, but it also covers a tour of duty in Vietnam near the end of the war.

Rick Spencer was a friend and I knew him well. He was a fun-loving hardworking guy who liked fast cars and rock 'n' roll. He went to Vietnam and served his country, only to return home a different man.

After all these years, I wanted to find out what really happened to him on that fall night in 1974.

This is his story.

Rick Spencer
1971 Senior Yearbook Photograph

Prologue

The '60s was one of the most tumultuous decades in the country's history and the youth of America were right in the middle of it. A lot of the discontent stemmed from the Vietnam War. During this time, the anti-establishment movement challenged patriotism, long hair replaced crewcuts, the Beatles took over the top spot on the music charts from the Beach Boys, and sex emerged from the bedroom and right out onto Main Street. Bell bottoms, ruffle-trimmed pastel-colored shirts, and wide ties became the style for the men, while the women gave up dresses and skirts for pantsuits, miniskirts, and jeans.

Desegregation made strides in some states to balance the scales of racism, while the assassinations of the Kennedy brothers and Martin Luther King shook the foundation of our democracy. The use of drugs spread throughout the country like wildfire. As the '70s arrived, the country and the world looked and acted differently.

By 1974, the United States was no longer actively involved in the Vietnam War and the country tried to adjust to life after the controversial conflict. Washington, D.C., was embroiled in the Watergate scandal and by August, it had forced Richard Nixon out of office, the first U.S. president ever to resign. Vice President Gerald Ford was sworn in to replace him.

Most college students didn't care much about Nixon, Watergate, or even the war. They wanted to get through school, land a job, and have a good time along the way.

Students in Chattanooga were typical—on a clear fall day in 1974. The season had been fairly warm. Nights were cool, but most days the temperatures bounced up into the 70s. Leaves were just beginning to change color and their beauty abounded in this part of East Tennessee. The humidity was low and a freshness was in the air.

Out in the middle of the Tennessee River, a cabin cruiser chugged peacefully downstream toward the Chickamauga Dam as a group of college-age kids, including my girlfriend Cindy and me, began arriving at a lake house that sat on the northern banks of Chickamauga Lake. There was nothing better than a party at the lake on a warm Saturday afternoon in October.

By midafternoon, about 30 kids were hanging out. Most were students at the University of Tennessee Chattanooga, but a few others were from nearby schools, and some weren't students at all, but just worked. The attendees spread out all over the property—in the house, on the patio in the backyard overlooking the lake, on the dock with their feet in the water. A couple even braved the chilly lake water as they took a quick dip. Whiskey and beer were abundant and at times, the smell of marijuana permeated the air.

The girls' conversations focused on school, while the boys talked about football. It was a day to put the daily grind of school or work out of mind and enjoy time with friends and cocktails and joints. About six p.m., our hostess was cooking hot dogs and hamburgers on the grill when the phone rang. I watched as the hostess ran into the house to answer it. She listened for a few moments, then laid the phone down on the counter and walked out onto the patio. When I saw that she was approaching me, I shook my head. No one knew where I was except Cindy, and she was sitting next to me.

"You have a call."

"Are you sure?" I replied.

"Yes. She said her name is Spencer."

Cindy asked, "Rick's mother?"

I shrugged. "The last I heard, Mrs. Spencer was living in Paris. If it is her, why would she be calling me? Let me go and see what this is about."

I walked inside, picked up the phone, and said, "Hello?"

"Buck, this is Lillie Spencer. Do you know where Rick is?"

I paused a moment to think about the question. Then I answered, "No ma'am. I haven't seen him in a couple of weeks or so."

She replied, "He's been missing for several days. As you know, I've been living in France and I aways call him on Sunday nights. When I called this past Sunday, his roommate told me he hadn't seen him since Thursday night. I got worried and flew back from Paris and I've been calling all over town looking for him."

I replied, "Well, Mrs. Spencer, I'm really sorry to hear this. And you can be sure that if I see him, I'll let you know."

She said, "Thanks," then hung up the phone.

I stood there with the phone in my hand looking out at the lake as I began to think about Rick. I finally returned the phone to the cradle, walked outside, and sat down next the Cindy. I didn't utter a word.

Finally, she asked, "Well, what did Mrs. Spencer want?"

I slowly replied, "She wanted to know if I knew where Rick was. I don't know where he is, but I have the strongest feeling that this isn't good. This isn't good at all."

Chapter 1—Who Was Rick Spencer?

Roderick Cason Spencer was born in Chattanooga on May 13, 1953. He was the only child of Lillie and Harry Spencer. Known from early in his life as Rick, he lived in the Woodmore, a middle-class section of Brainerd, and had attended Woodmore Elementary School. Harry was a businessman and Lillie was a musician who played the piano and organ; she loved music. Rick followed his mother's passion for music. He sang in the youth choir at Central Baptist Church of Woodmore and learned to play the piano when he was very young. Music came naturally to him.

By the time he got to junior-high school, he was playing organ in rock 'n' roll bands and was still involved with music at the church.

Growing up, Rick was a likable kid, with a quick wit. He normally had a smile on his face. Thus, he had no shortage of friends. He was an average student in school, but was very industrious and not afraid to work. Rick cut lawns and did odd jobs for neighbors. While attending Dalewood Junior High School, he began working part-time at Drew's Drugs, a store in Dalewood. He was thrifty with his money and saved it, hoping to buy a car when he got to be 16.

It was at Dalewood Junior High where I met Rick. We had gone to different elementary schools. We had a couple of classes together at Dalewood and soon became good friends. My dad took us to high-school football games.

My father was an avid hunter and loved guns. On most Sunday afternoons, he and I went shooting at the Chattanooga

Rifle Club where we were members. During one of the football games, my dad asked Rick if he'd like to go shooting sometime.

Rick said, "Sure!" He'd never shot guns before.

A few weeks later on a Sunday afternoon, we picked up Rick at his house in Woodmore and were off to the Rifle Club. After just one session of shooting, Rick was hooked. He was fascinated with guns and wanted to know all he could about them. Virtually every time the Buchanans went to the Rifle Club, we invited Rick, and he didn't miss many opportunities to handle pistols, rifles, and shotguns.

Over the next several months, my dad showed Rick the ABCs of guns, which covered gun safety, cleaning, and how to shoot all types. It wasn't long before he became a very good shot with a rifle.

Rick's father, Harry, died in 1969, which left Lillie to raise her high-school-aged son alone. She was lucky: Rick was a good kid. He behaved in class, got decent grades, and held down an after-school job at Drew's Drugs. Rick was zoned to attend Brainerd High School, which was just a mile or so from his house, but he opted to go all the way across town, some 10 miles each way, to attend Chattanooga High School, commonly known as City High. Part of the reason was that as soon as he was old enough to get his license, he could drive to and from school in one of the family cars, a sleek beige-colored 1963 Dodge Dart.

The Dodge had an automatic transmission, but with a push-button gear shift on the dashboard, while most cars had the gear shifts attached to the steering wheel or mounted to the floor. There were six silver buttons: park, reverse, neutral, first, second, and third. As he drove across town, Rick pushed those buttons like a race car driver. Of course, since it was an automatic, he didn't need the buttons to shift the gears, but he pushed them anyway. He let the engine whine as he went from first to second and finally into third. He felt this method allowed him to maximize the speed he could coax out of the brown beauty.

One of the drawbacks of attending City High was that Rick didn't know too many kids, so he had to make a new set of friends. His wit, charm, and smile allowed him to do that in almost all cases. One particular case stood out. He'd been there only a couple of weeks when he found himself in the boy's bathroom with the class bully, who was also in his homeroom. The bully, a football and basketball player, was six-four and weighed about 230 pounds. Rick was about six feet tall and weighed 150.

The tormentor backed Rick against the wall and said, "I don't like the way you laugh. It gets on my nerves in homeroom!"

Rick was no match for him physically, but his quick wit allowed him to talk his way out of getting beat up. He won over the big guy and from that day on, he never had a problem with the bully.

I ended up going to City High in my junior and senior years, but since I participated in sports, Rick and I didn't see much of each other. He was an average student at City High.

Throughout high school, Rick kept working at the drug store and continued to play rock and roll. He didn't have time for any extracurricular activities, other than attending a few sporting events. He did find time to cruise Shoney's Restaurant, looking for girls and a street race.

Cruising Shoney's

Shoney's, on Brainerd Road, the main drag in this part of Chattanooga, was the place to be most nights. This particular location was a drive-in restaurant where cars pulled into the parking spots and placed their order on an intercom system. The food was delivered by a cute bell-hop girl wearing black pants, a white shirt with a black string tie, and a white server's hat with "Shoney's" written in script on the side.

While the burgers, fries, milkshakes, and strawberry pies were tasty, Shoney's was best known as a pickup place for high-school kids. Guys and gals cruised around the parking lot looking for each other. Occasionally, one found another, but mainly it was the place to be seen. Rick was a regular; he was always looking for a date or a late-night race on I-75.

He loved cruising the parking lot, even in his nearly 10-year-old beige Dodge. Hanging out the window, he yelled at friends or potential racing opponents as he pushed the neutral button and gunned the engine of the aging car. Observing his mannerisms, one would have thought he was touring in a brand-new GTO instead of the dated Dodge.

The sedan didn't look like it could get up too much speed, but surprisingly, it had a V-8 engine, which gave it an unexpected amount of pep. Rick was always open to a race from any challenger and Shoney's was the place to find one; all the boys went there to show off their cars. And he took them all on. The high-performance cars, like the Shelbys, the 442 Chevelles, and the Plymouth GTXs, didn't pay him much attention, but the Mustangs and Camaros sometimes went up against him just for kicks. The boys who drove the fast cars were either gearheads or rich kids and most came from nearby high schools, such as Brainerd, East Ridge, Tyner, or Lakeview. The racers thought it was way to attract the girls; winning a race might also mean getting a date. Simply put, the thrill of the speed and the testosterone drove the competition.

The street races took place after nine p.m. on I-75. They started at East Brainerd Road and finished near the Eastgate Shopping Mall just before the interstate split, I-75 heading south to Georgia and I-24 leading northwest toward downtown Chattanooga and Lookout Mountain. Everyone around Brainerd that had a fast car and wanted to race knew the route. On occasion, the police were waiting, on hand to issue a hefty fine if a racer was caught.

It was a short drive from Shoney's. The racers typically followed one another to the entrance ramp to the interstate. Once they reached the ramp, they sat there until no cars were in sight. Then they slowly drove onto the freeway, lined up side by side, and began a slow rolling start. Once they reached the mile marker just past East Brained Road, it was hammer-down time.

They raced until they reached the next mile marker and whoever got there first was the winner. After the race, the contestants returned to Shoney's where the victor took a victory lap. Rick didn't win many races, but he never backed down from a chance to see what the beige Dodge could do. He loved the speed and the thrill of the race.

Adding up Shoney's, school, and work, Rick's trips to the gun range became fewer and fewer, but his love for guns didn't wane. As a matter of fact, he bought a couple of guns and had his own membership in the Chattanooga Rifle Club.

There at the Club, Rick met Joe Dyer.

Joe, also a gun enthusiast, had graduated from East Ridge High School in 1968. Rick and Joe met there occasionally for an afternoon of target shooting.

Rick's three years at City High were uneventful. He graduated in the spring of 1971. While he'd taken all the core classes, what benefitted him the most was that he'd learned how to take care of himself. Growing up without a father in the house and a mother who had to work, Rick had no choice but to fend for himself, whether it was maintaining his car, making and saving money, buying groceries, cooking meals, cleaning up the house, standing up to bullies, or dealing with people. He wound up with a reputation as a diligent worker and somewhat of an entrepreneur. Rick was clearly driven by success and prosperity, which in part was a result of growing up without a father

With his high-school diploma in hand, he enrolled at the local college, the University of Tennessee at Chattanooga (UTC).

UTC

As Rick prepared for his freshman year of college, he continued to live at home with his mother. He'd finally quit his job at the drug store and began working for two ladies who owned a carpet shop. One of the ladies went to Rick's church and had known him since he was a child. She knew he had a good work ethic. They sold carpet and provided a carpet-cleaning service. The store was full of displays featuring a variety of types and colors of carpeting.

Rick was their jack of all trades. He picked up carpet at wholesalers and delivered it to retail buyers, cleaned carpets for customers, and even manned the store when the owners were away. He liked working there; he could put in lots of hours and made more money than at the drug store. In a short period of time, Rick had proven to the ladies that he was dependable and trustworthy.

One of their customers was the Town and Country Restaurant in North Chattanooga. It was one of the nicer restaurants in that part of town. Once every three or four months, Rick and a helper showed up after hours with their cleaning equipment. They moved all the tables and chairs, then cleaned the carpets and moved all the furniture back in place. When they were finished, which was normally between one and two o'clock in the morning, Rick locked up the place and headed home. The manager had given him a key and told him to keep it.

In September 1971, Rick started classes at UTC. He planned to major in business and took a basic freshman workload. He was diligent about attending class, but like all college kids, he missed a class or two.

As summer turned to fall, he'd saved up enough money to buy a new bright-red 1971 Dodge 340 Dart Swinger. He no longer had to push buttons on the console to shift gears. His new car also had an automatic transmission, but the shift stick was on the floor like most cars of the day. To be sure, he still shifted the gears as he drove around town. The red Dodge could really fly, and he was now a serious threat on the I-75 race circuit. But his busy schedule allowed little time for the Shoney's visits and street racing.

Since graduating from City High, his music career had slowed down. He was no longer a member of a band, but he filled in if a group needed a keyboard player on the weekends. Rick saw that working for the carpet ladies was much more profitable than playing rock and roll.

In his little bit of spare time, he occasionally went out on a date or to a party. This was where his most interesting traits revealed themselves. Rick didn't drink, which was very surprising for an outgoing guy like him; virtually everyone drank and when Rick was a senior in high school, the state of Tennessee lowered the drinking age from 21 to 18. This was in response to an argument that a young man could go to Vietnam at 18, but couldn't legally drink.

Rick also didn't smoke or have anything to do with drugs. This, too, was highly unusual for college kids and musicians. His only real vice was that he let out an occasional curse word.

So he went to parties just for the social aspect. Rick liked being with friends and entertained them by telling stories or playing practical jokes on an unexpected buddy. Sometimes the jokes got him in trouble, especially when the recipient didn't see the same level of humor in the prank that Rick did. But he always managed to talk or laugh his way out of any retribution by the victim.

On Sundays, it wasn't unusual for him to go to church with his mom. Sometimes he helped with the music program.

All in all, Rick Spencer was pretty much a fun-loving straight-arrow kid who mostly liked to work and make money.

One night, he was on a carpet-cleaning job at a store in a strip shopping center. He finished around 11:30 p.m. and loaded up his equipment in the company's van. As he went to the get into the van, he noticed that next door to the store was an U.S. Army recruiting office. He stared at it for a minute, then started up the van, pulled out of the parking lot, and headed home.

On his way home he began to think about the Army.

At this time, while the Vietnam War was winding down, military service wasn't very popular, but that didn't faze Rick. After all, he liked guns and if Uncle Sam needed him to go, he would. As he thought about it, he considered himself a true American, unlike those long-haired hippies who protested the war. At 18, he'd be eligible for the draft in a year. In the meantime, he asked himself, why not find out what the Army was all about?

"Tell Me About the Army"

The next day after class, Rick drove back to the recruiting office. Walking in, he saw a gray-painted wooden desk where a staff sergeant with a crewcut and dressed in olive-green fatigues was sitting. The soldier stood and greeted Rick, then asked if he could help him.

Rick replied, "Tell me about the Army."

The sergeant invited Rick to have a seat in a wooden chair in front of the desk.

As Rick sat down, the sergeant pulled out a pack of Pall Mall cigarettes. He offered one to his guest, but Rick declined. Next, he pulled out one of the non-filtered cigarettes and tapped the end of it on the table a couple of times before placing it in his mouth and holding it between his lips. Then he casually pulled out a Zippo lighter from his pants pocket. There was a metallic click as he flipped open the silver case and rolled the striker back with his thumb and suddenly a yellow-blue flame appeared. He lit the cigarette and snapped the lighter shut with another clicking sound as he took a drag off the cigarette. A second later, he blew streams of smoke out of his nose. Though Rick didn't smoke, he was impressed with the precise manner in which the soldier undertook this routine task, almost as if it had been a regular drill in Basic Training. He then put the smoking cigarette in a square glass ashtray and started telling Rick about the Army.

The recruiter had been in the Army for 10 years and served two tours of duty in Vietnam. He explained to Rick about Army life and covered the steps, from Basic Training to duty assignments. At that time, there were primarily three places where a recruit would be assigned: stateside, Europe, or Vietnam. Spencer had a lot of questions about Vietnam and the sergeant shared his experience with Rick.

While the U.S. was reducing the number of troops in Nam, replacements were still needed as soldiers finished out their tours of duty. The Army's main group, the infantry, was being phased out and replaced by South Vietnamese troops. The U.S. Army still needed support troops, such as mechanics, medics, and communications and logistics personnel. They also needed helicopter pilots and crews. This piqued Rick's interest and he wanted to know more. The sergeant told Rick that if he made the cut, he could fly a Huey with a crew of four, one being a door gunner.

Rick asked about the gunner's job.

The sergeant told him, "It's like the guy who rode shotgun on the stagecoach in the old western movies. It's his job to protect the aircraft, but instead of using a shotgun, the gunner mans a machine gun." The crewcut soldier continued, "U.S. Army helicopters ferry troops to and from the battlefield regardless of if they're American or South Vietnamese. They also resupply them whenever necessary."

After the discussion about Vietnam, the staff sergeant explained the benefits of joining the Army. He outlined the career and the single-tour options. One thing that got Rick's attention was the GI Bill. If a serviceman received an honorable discharge, the GI Bill would fundamentally pay for his college education. Always money conscience, Rick liked the sound of that.

After about an hour-and-a-half discussion, Rick thanked the sergeant. The men stood up and shook hands. Rick told him he'd be back in touch in a week or so. He went out the door and headed to his red Dodge. He had a lot to think about.

Chapter 2—Vietnam

Rick, like most Americans, had been watching the Vietnam War on the nightly news since he was in junior-high school, but he didn't really know a lot about it. The day after his visit to the recruiter, he went to the school library, read up on it, and quickly came away with a better understanding of the Southeast Asian country and conflict.

Vietnam had been a French colony since the late nineteenth century. It was part of what was called French Indochina, which also at the time included the countries of Cambodia and Laos.

Most of Indochina was occupied by the Japanese during World War II. After Japan was defeated, the French reclaimed the area, but they'd been greatly weakened by World War II, which affected their ability to control the region. Cambodia and Laos became independent of France in the early '50s, while the French continued their rule over Vietnam. The French had been fighting resistance guerrillas, called the Viet Minh, almost since the end of the Second World War. By the mid-'50s, after the decisive battle at Dien Bien Phu in 1954, in which 50,000 French paratroopers found themselves surrounded by the Vietnamese (upwards of 20,000 were either killed, wounded, or taken prisoner), France determined it'd had enough of Indochina and withdrew from the region.

As a result of the French's exit, Vietnam was split in two. North Vietnam evolved as a communist country supported by the Soviet Union and China. South Vietnam became a democratic nation backed by the United States. The Viet Minh evolved into the North's Communist Party, while and the communist Viet Cong launched a guerilla insurgency in the

11

South, fomenting a civil war and fighting the South Vietnamese military.

The Vietnam War, as waged by the U.S., was a fight between different ideologies. It was communism versus democracy and none of the global powers wanted to lose. The U.S. strategy was to provide the South with money, armaments, and military advisors. When President Dwight Eisenhower left office in 1961, fewer than 1,000 U.S. military advisors were in Vietnam. Under the Kennedy administration, the number grew to more than 15,000.

After President Kennedy was assassinated in November 1963, Lyndon Johnson became the 36th president. He escalated the war to a whole new level. In the spring of 1965, the first American combat soldiers saw action when an entire battalion of U.S. Marines landed near Da Nang, a South Vietnamese city on the eastern coast of the country. At the time, the American people fully supported the incursion. By December 1965, Johnson had increased the number of American military personnel to 200,000.

As the number of U.S. ground troops increased, a demilitarized zone (DMZ) was established along the 17th parallel between North Vietnam and South Vietnam. The U.S. military was instructed by the politicians not to send ground troops north of the DMZ or into neutral Cambodia and Laos, both west of Vietnam. In essence, we were helping to defend South Vietnam, rather than to win an offensive war.

This strategy was similar to the way the U.S. fought the Korean War a decade earlier. The reasoning in both the Korean and the Vietnam conflicts was to avoid, at all costs, having the war bleed into China, which could potentially lead to another World War. China borders northern Korea, as well as Vietnam and Laos.

Also like the Korean War, the objectives of the Vietnam War were hard to define. This was completely opposite to

World War II where the objectives couldn't be clearer: defeat Germany in Europe and Japan in the Pacific. That was an offensive war to end all wars, with the Allies hitting the Nazis on all fronts—France, Italy, North Africa, and Russia—to close in on Germany and capturing island after island in the Pacific, each victory getting closer to Japan.

The defensive policy for Vietnam was also opposite to the way the American military officers had been trained. West Point and the other U.S. military institutions taught that the way to win wars was to take it to the enemy with offensive tactics. In Vietnam, all the armed forces were mandated by Congress to follow defensive guidelines. The communists in the north and the insurgents in the south, meanwhile, played by their own rules. As a result, the ground battles were mostly fought in the South.

The North moved troops and supplies unabated into South Vietnam via jungle trails that ran through Cambodia and Laos. This supply line was referred to as the Ho Chi Minh Trail, named for the Vietnamese revolutionary and statesman who was prime minister and president of the unified country, ruling from Hanoi in North Vietnam. Over time, bombing was allowed beyond the DMZ and into the bordering countries, but ground-troop offensives remained taboo. The foot soldier had to stay within the borders of South Vietnam and defend the country.

The North's army was well trained, well equipped, and supported by the Soviets. They employed both conventional and guerilla tactics. They also backed the Viet Cong in its guerilla insurgency against the South Vietnam and U.S. militaries.

It was easy to distinguish between the two fighting forces that became our enemies in the Vietnam War. The North wore uniforms and looked like soldiers, while the Cong dressed like the civilians and blended in with the non-combatant population. Thus, the Americans faced a dual challenge, one on the battlefront as they faced an experienced foe with an aggressive strategy, the other a deadly grass-roots and underground movement conducted by an often-invisible adversary.

But after a short while, the Americans set up their own strategy, which was referred to as "Search and Destroy." In other words, hunt down and eliminate the enemy. The American plan was working and by the end of 1967, it appeared that they were gaining the upper hand. The end of the war was within sight.

That all changed in late January 1968, when the communists launched the Tet Offensive. More than 80,000 North Vietnamese and Viet Cong engaged in a well-orchestrated surprise attack on 100 or more targets in the South. After about 90 days, the Americans and South Vietnamese turned the tide and beat back the offensive, but the price was extraordinarily high, both in terms of American losses and public sentiment. Before Tet, the U.S. public support for the war was more than 50 percent. After the attack, it dropped into the low 30s.

The Americans and the world knew that if the communists could launch such a widespread offensive, the war was far from over. The public and the media turned against the war, while the military demanded more troops. By the spring of 1969, the number of U.S. soldiers on the ground in Vietnam had risen to over 540,000. Many of the troops, especially the grunts on the front lines, had been conscripted. The draft put all young men between the ages of 18 and around 29 in jeopardy of being called up and sent to the war against their will. Many received deferments by attending college, some fled to Canada and other countries, a few went to jail as conscientious objectors, some got married and had kids right away, and the rest got out with various medical conditions. Basically, the more money you had, the easier it was to avoid the draft. But that put the onus of fighting the war on the least advantaged young men in the country.

In the meantime, in a political shocker, in 1967 during the major escalation of the war from the American side, President Johnson opted not to run for reelection in 1968. Richard Nixon defeated Hubert Humphrey, LBJ's vice president, and assumed office in January 1969. One of his campaign promises was to end the war in Vietnam. After only a few months in office, he ordered the withdrawal of 150,000 U.S. troops. Nixon's strategy was to transfer the fighting responsibilities to the South Vietnamese Army. This was referred to as "Vietnamization." Over the next couple of years, the U.S. removed most of the combat troops, but kept support units. However, replacements were still needed.

Politicians always play a part in war, but in this conflict, Congress seemed to have more say than in other wars. This put added pressure on the military leaders, who also faced challenges from three relatively new wartime influencers. The Vietnam War became the first televised war, anti-war protests popped up across the U.S., and drugs were prevalent among the troops.

Television: The Nightly War at 6 p.m.

Ten years earlier as the '60s began, most U.S. households already had televisions, which had replaced the radio as the mass medium for news and entertainment. The Vietnam War was televised on the nightly news broadcasts to the extent that it became must-watch TV. More often than not, the field reports provided footage of combat and the carnage of war, along with the casualty count for the day. People at home could sit on their couches and watch the war.

World War II had been filmed and movie theaters across the country played newsreels weekly, but the content was controlled by the military. All the news from the war zones was censored by the government. The clips mainly showed positive events and when bad news was reported, it was typically with an optimistic spin. The overall goal was to keep the folks back home informed, but in good spirits to maintain their support.

During the Vietnam War, the government's censorship efforts were much more lax. News crews were in the combat zones non-stop. Reporters submitted daily dispatches on exactly what they'd witnessed in the field. They reported the good as well as the bad, which gave the American public a more realistic view of what was going on in the jungles of Southeast Asia. Thus, the three national television networks, ABC, CBS, and NBC, reported what they wanted with their own twist. As the war dragged on, this became more problematic for the military and the government. Public support for the war continued to dwindle and this widened the major fracture in American society.

Protest and Unrest

At the beginning of the '60s, the U.S. military was highly regarded throughout the country, thanks to its efforts in World War II, but by the end of the decade, that had all changed. The Tet Offensive was the catalyst. It was a military defeat for the communists, but it became a public-relations nightmare for the Americans.

The public now felt that this war was far from over and their hunch was confirmed on TV a few weeks later when the generals asked for another 200,000 troops to be deployed to Vietnam. These events kicked the anti-war sentiment, which seemed to have reached a peak during the Democratic National Convention in Chicago in late August 1968, into an even higher gear. More violent protests, especially in Washington, D.C., along with the non-violent peace movement eroded what little support remained with the military. By 1970, only 3% of enlisted soldiers selected combat assignments. Even the once-robust ROTC programs at high schools and colleges across the county saw their enrollments cut in half.

The American public was growing tired of the war and were horrified by what they were seeing on the nightly news. This further exacerbated the fault lines dividing the country between the anti-establishment counterculture and the equally passionate "love-it-or-leave-it" patriotic side.

Unfortunately for the returning soldiers, they became a symbol of the earthquake fracturing the nation. In the past, returning soldiers were cheered and celebrated as conquering heroes, but that wasn't the case for this war. GIs returning from Vietnam were ridiculed, insulted, and blatantly mistreated.

Anti-war protests gripped almost every major city and many college campuses. Thousands of protestors, young and old, demanded an end to the war and an immediate withdrawal of all troops.

The frenzy reached a pinnacle in 1970 at Kent State University in Ohio. The National Guard was called out to control an on-campus demonstration. The crowd got out of hand, the soldiers reacted, and they fired more than 60 rounds at the students in less than 15 seconds. When the smoke cleared, four students lay dead and nine others were wounded. The morale of the soldiers and the American public was now at an all-time low.

The counterculture became more visible in the late sixties, but it had been evolving since the American combat troops

17

first went to Vietnam. Some believed that the use of drugs had aided in the changing culture and a part of this fell squarely on the shoulders of the U.S. military.

Drugs in War

A significant element to the young counterculture was the explosion of the use of recreational drugs, most of which were illegal. This situation was, in part, fueled by drugs prescribed at times for combat soldiers. Military doctors supplied them with amphetamines for bursts of energy and courage during combat and for long missions to help their endurance; sedatives were provided to help relieve anxiety due to the stress of war and to titrate down from the speed. The acceptance of these prescribed drugs opened the door for recreational drugs; it showed that drug use was acceptable and non-prescribed illegal drugs were readily available.

In previous wars, alcohol had long been an answer to battle fatigue, but in Vietnam, marijuana was readily available and served the same purpose. Grown in the country, as well as all over Southeast Asia, cannabis and hashish were widely used. It was easy for soldiers to score in villages or towns. Some estimates found that by 1970, more than 50% of the soldiers in the war-torn country were using marijuana. Local pot was also so inexpensive, it could be bartered for as little as a pack of cigarettes.

In addition, Vietnam is one of the countries within the Golden Triangle, where opium was (and is) a major cash crop and heroin and other narcotics were abundant and cheap. In fact, heroin was the second most popular drug. Cocaine and hallucinogenic drugs such as LSD were also used. Drugs were abundant in the country. In some cases, drugs were easier to obtain than beer and whiskey.

As the support of the war continued to wane, the morale of the soldiers went with it; this also contributed to an increase in drug use. Drugs had become a big problem for the military and they had to put plans in place to deal with it.

In addition to all the peace and anti-establishment movements, the draft was winding down. Still, the Army needed soldiers and a number of young men were willing to serve.

A Made-Up Mind

It was early December 1971. The first semester of classes was coming to an end and Rick had finished his final test of the year. If he was going back to school in January, it was time for him to register for the winter term. However, he'd been weighing his options, which were to go to school or to join the Army. It had been a couple of weeks since Rick had first met with the recruiting sergeant. He'd talked to his mother about his meeting and as you would expect, she was adamantly opposed to him enlisting.

Neither Lillie's objections nor the bad press about Vietnam, the protests, the disrespect for the war veterans deterred Rick. He made up his mind to join the Army and volunteer for Vietnam as a door gunner on a helicopter. What the recruiting sergeant didn't tell him was that door gunners had one of the highest mortality rates of any position in combat. Indeed, the door gunner was among the most vulnerable combatant, given his almost complete exposure to enemy fire, especially with helicopters being a prime target of ground forces. At the worst of the fighting, door gunners had a life expectancy of 15-30 days. But Rick knew none of this when he volunteered. So he wasn't particularly worried about coming back. He was confident that he'd make it home. He'd return to school and use the GI Bill to pay for his education. But at this point in time, school wasn't really on his mind. He wanted to get in on the action in Southeast Asia before the war was over.

He went back to the recruiting office and officially signed up. He was scheduled to report to Basic Training in February 1972. That night at dinner, he told his mom of his decision. Broken-hearted, she left the dinner table, went to her bedroom, and wept for most of the night. She'd lost her husband only a few years ago and couldn't face the prospect of losing her only child as well.

Rick cleaned up the kitchen and headed out to meet a few friends.

He met them at Shakey's Pizza on Brainerd Road just across from Shoney's. When he first told them about joining the Army, they didn't believe him. They knew full well that Vietnam and the military were hugely unpopular. Returning servicemen were urged by their superiors to wear civilian clothes rather than their uniforms as they departed the military bases. Otherwise, they would draw the wrath of protestors. But Rick kept on insisting that he wasn't kidding. They all told him he was nuts, but even that didn't change his mind.

On Christmas Eve, Rick went to church with his mother. By now, most of his friends and church members knew about his commitment to enlist. All wished him the best and said they would keep him in their prayers. As New Year's 1972 rolled around, he had less than two months before the first leg of his military journey. Until then, he spent his time working for the carpet ladies. The time flew by and before Rick knew it, it was time to be on his way to Basic Training.

With his Army orders in hand, Rick hugged his mother one last time before he boarded the Greyhound Bus at the downtown Chattanooga station on Market Street. He took a seat next to the window and waved goodbye to Lillie as the bus pulled out of the station. He was on his way to Columbus, Georgia, to do his basic training at Fort Benning. The tall, thin, shaggy-headed boy from Chattanooga, Tennessee, was in the Army now. Little did he know his life would never be the same.

Chapter 3—In the Army Now

At Fort Benning, Rick was given a new-style haircut and wardrobe. A buzz cut took the place of his wavy hair and his blue jeans and T-shirts were swapped for Army-issue green shirts and pants. His tennis shoes were exchanged for black boots.

Rick was determined to be a good soldier and knew it would begin with Basic. Although he struggled with some of the physical activities, such as exercising and running, he stuck with it and became an ideal recruit. By the time he got to the rifle range, it seemed like he'd marched or run 500 miles. He was looking forward to the shooting part of the training and here his time at the Chattanooga Rifle Club paid off; he quickly rose to the head of the class for his marksmanship skills.

He completed Basic Training in eight weeks, then put in another four weeks in Advanced Individual Training (AIT), where he spent most of his time at the gun range handling machine guns, M16 rifles, and pistols. It didn't take long for him to get the hang of firing a machine gun and once again, he got high marks for marksmanship. With his training complete, he was issued his orders: the combat zone in Vietnam. Before he shipped out across the Pacific, he was given leave to return home.

Off to Southeast Asia

Lillie Spencer was delighted to see her son, but it was a short visit and by the middle of May, Rick was on a plane with the other replacements and headed to Southeast Asia. It was a long day. He left Chattanooga, changed planes in Atlanta, then flew to Seattle, where he and the other soldiers boarded another commercial jet headed to their destination: Saigon, Vietnam. He didn't sleep much on the plane and by the time they landed near the South Vietnamese capital city, he was dog tired.

As he stepped onto the portable stairway that led from the plane onto the tarmac, he gasped as he felt the oppressive heat and humidity. The temperature was only in the 80s, but with the humidity it felt more like 90-plus. After he retrieved his gear, he was ordered onto one of the buses out in front of the terminal. It was an olive-green school bus and had metal bars over the windows.

He threw his duffel bag in the trailer hooked up behind the bus and boarded. Rick asked the driver about the bars protecting the windows.

He replied in a matter-of-fact voice, "It's to prevent some of the natives from throwing grenades inside."

"Oh, thanks." Rick found a seat, sat down, and before the bus got rolling was sound asleep.

The bus traveled an hour or so north to the in-country processing center where new arrivals were given time to acclimate to Vietnam. This included getting used to the time change, weather, country, enemy, and dos and don'ts.

Rick woke up when the bus stopped. At the center, he and the others were issued their new jungle fatigues, caps, and boots. He was assigned a barracks, bed, and locker and given a schedule for the next two days. Interspersed with resting time, he was required to attend several talks about life in-country.

On his third day, he was told to get his gear; he was moving out. Most of the other replacements had to wait about a week or so for their assignments, but not Rick. He was given his orders, boarded another green Army school bus, and was off to join his unit. He would be reporting to an aviation company.

He'd gotten his wish to be a door gunner on an assault helicopter.

Upon arrival at the base, he disembarked from the bus and reported to the duty sergeant, who told him to report to his platoon leader and gave him directions to his living quarters. After a brief discussion with his reporting officer, Rick headed over to his quarters. It was a wooden structure with screen-covered windows and a tin roof. Sandbags were stacked around all sides of the building up to just below the windows, which were at the top of the walls.

The hooch, as it was called, was big enough to sleep six men. It had a dirt floor and single bunks, footlockers, tables, and chairs neatly lined up around the room. In one of the corners sat a refrigerator and a table with a stereo. A couple of swirling fans attached to the walls tried to move the humid air.

As Rick entered, he met a couple of his hooch mates, one of whom pointed to his bed. He was also introduced to their hooch maid, a Vietnamese lady whose job was to clean the room and wash the soldiers' clothes. She was short, less than five feet tall, and Rick thought she looked to be in her early teens, but he found out later that she was 25. He thought, "This tour can't be that bad if we have our own maid."

When Rick reached Southeast Asia, the United States's military involvement was nothing like it had been just a year earlier. Nixon's Vietnamization strategy was in full swing and the South Vietnam Army had taken over most of the ground fighting and defensive positions. The American forces were being phased out and had been reduced from a high of 540,000 to around 50,000 troops. Only U.S. support units were left in the country. The helicopters were mainly used to ferry South Vietnamese troops and supplies into landing zones. There were also some reconnaissance and rescue missions.

After Rick got settled in, he spent the next six days being trained on a helicopter. After his first breakfast at the mess hall, he was walking back to his hooch. He paused for a minute as he glazed off in the distance at the green mountains of Vietnam. They somewhat reminded him of the Smoky Mountains of eastern Tennessee, but Rick would be a very different man the next time he saw the beauty of his home state.

After a week in Vietnam, the honeymoon was over. Rick was going on his first mission. The day before he was scheduled to take off, he met with the crew and attended the briefing to review their assignment. He was assigned to a Bell UH-1C Iroquois helicopter, otherwise called a Huey. The Huey was the most versatile and popular aircraft used during the Vietnam War and many thought it was the best when it came to jungle warfare.

It required a crew of four, which included the aircraft commander (AC), pilot, crew chief, and door gunner. The crew chief was responsible for the helicopter; it was his baby and his job to make sure it was ready for battle every time it took off. He also served as a door gunner.

The crew chief and the door gunners each had an M60 machine gun, which fired a 7.62mm-caliber shell at a rate of up to 700 rounds per minute. The gunners were also issued an M16 rifle and a 38-caliber pistol, which was carried in belt-attached holsters. They had to carry these weapons with them anytime they left the chopper. Most Hueys were also equipped with rocket launchers, along with miniguns that were a modern version of a Gatling gun. Needless to say, they had a lot of firepower.

The AC's job was to command the aircraft and give orders to the crew. He told the gunners when to start and stop firing during a mission. He was also in constant contact with the flight leader, who commanded all the helicopters on the assigned mission.

The gunner's task was to protect the aircraft, as well as the other aircraft and troops. On most missions, the gunner used his machine gun to lay down suppressive fire to keep the enemy under cover as helicopters delivered troops or supplies into a landing zone.

The company's planning and scheduling had been done and Rick's crew had been briefed. Their mission would be to drop off South Vietnamese troops in the designated area of operation. Each chopper could carry five soldiers in addition to its flight crew. The crew would be taking off in the morning at sunrise.

Under Fire

After dinner, Rick went back to the hooch and played some cards with his hooch mates. He was offered a beer, but refused. He was shocked when he was asked if he wanted to smoke pot; again, he refused. Wanting to get a good night's rest for the early mission, he turned in early. Once he lay down on his bunk, the butterflies began to flutter in his belly. Obviously, they came from the anticipation and unknown of his first mission, where he might come under fire.

Hell, he was afraid. It could very well be his last night on Earth. He had little idea what to expect. Since arriving in Southeast Asia, he'd heard a number of stories from his hooch mates about missions that they'd flown. Starting tomorrow, he'd have his own story to tell.

Rick didn't sleep at all that night and the next morning; he was ready to go before anyone else. After breakfast, a truck picked up the soldiers from the company area and took them to the flight line where their big bird awaited. The AC led the way to their assigned aircraft. Rick and the rest of the crew

26

followed. His job was to load 4,000 rounds of ammunition for the two door guns. He also made sure that each M60 was clean and in good working order. Next, he loaded each gun with a belt of ammunition.

The pilot went through the preflight check list. As he did, Rick buckled up in the monkey strap, a safety line attached to the helicopter to prevent the gunner from falling out.

Finally, Rick and the crew were ready. As he waited for takeoff, he felt like his heart was beating about 600 miles an hour and at any minute would jump right out of his chest.

It was still dark when Rick's chopper was given the up command and the Huey lifted off from the runway. It was one of six helicopters assigned to the mission. It took about 20 minutes to arrive at the pick-up zone, where each bird loaded five waiting South Vietnamese soldiers. Once they were in and buckled up, the big green birds took off and flew in a "V" formation as they headed toward the designated landing zone.

As they passed over the dense jungle, Rick noticed that his heart rate had slowed down, but the palms of his hand were clammy and he was sweating, not from the humidity, but from nerves. He was flying into battle for the first time and was worried about whether he could perform under fire. His shooting skills weren't under question; he knew he'd received excellent marksmanship ratings at every training stop.

Rick told himself to focus on the mission. He blocked everything else out of his mind and concentrated on watching the terrain below. He became so focused that he didn't hear the whine of the helicopter's turbines as the blades beat the air into submission.

Rick's concentration was broken when the AC announced over the intercom that they were five minutes away from the landing zone. He could see a clearing in the trees just up ahead where the first Huey was beginning to touch down to unload its troops. As they got closer to the clearing, Rick began to hear "pop pop." At first, he thought there was something wrong with the chopper; then he realized that it was small-arms fire hitting the aircraft.

A moment later, the AC gave the "hot" command, which meant the door gunners could engage the enemy at will. Rick could see the enemy coming out of the jungle into the open field. Though this was Rick's first time shooting at another human being, he didn't hesitate. He flipped off the safety, pulled back the bolt, and began to fire.

The next few minutes went by in a blur. He could see Viet Cong in the distance firing at the helicopters as they landed and discharged the troops. Rick laid down suppression fire as he tried to provide cover for the disembarking South Vietnamese. Bullets continued to hit the Huey during the landing. Fortunately, there was no major damage and not a scratch on any of the crew. The AC gave the cease-fire order as they pulled up, banked to the east, and headed back to base.

On the way back, Rick sat in the Huey's doorway with his feet dangling out, still secured with the monkey strap. He relived the skirmish in his mind. He didn't know how many he'd killed, but he'd seen them falling as the M60 bullets cut them to pieces. What amazed him was that despite the hail of bullets and their fallen comrades, they kept coming into the landing zone.

After refueling, Rick's crew repeated the mission. Once again, they returned unscathed.

The next day, there was another assignment, but this time, two out of the six Hueys didn't come back. Rick witnessed both incidents from his position in the door. One had been hit with a mortar round while landing and the other had crashed upon approach as both the pilot and the AC had been killed by machine-gun fire. He knew most of the guys on the downed aircrafts. Now he'd witnessed the death of people he knew, and that image would stay with him.

Rick had experienced war up close and personal. As his tour of duty continued, he flew six days a week with one off day. The missions had been for the most part reduced to only one per day. Most lasted less than five hours from liftoff to return. Only a year earlier it was not uncommon for Huey crews to fly 10-12 hours a day, seven days a week.

Rick and his hooch mates were spending more time in the hooch than in the air. Boredom was a problem. The down time only made a soldier miss home that much more.

Regardless of the mission, Rick took great pride in protecting his aircraft and its crew, but the stress of war was beginning to get to him. Add this to the idle time he had, and he looked for something to take his mind off the world. Beer, whiskey, and marijuana were readily available in the hooch. A few weeks earlier after a near-death experience, he finally broke down and took his first sip of alcohol. It wasn't long before it became a daily ritual after returning from an assignment.

The escape from reality didn't stop with the booze. He next ventured into the world of drugs. Rick tried marijuana and added it to his routine, but he avoided the harder drugs and hallucinogens. He was amazed by how easy the pot was to get. All he had to do was to order it from the hooch maid and she brought it to him the next day.

This was a young man who, though growing up in the '60s, had never experienced alcohol or marijuana before going to Southeast Asia. Rick was now indulging in both as he tried to escape the horrors of war and the boredom of being stationed in the jungle. But the horrors were far from over.

WIA

It had been over three months since Rick's maiden flight in Vietnam and by now, he'd become numb to daily war. It was, actually, routine. He no longer thought about flying into a combat zone and of killing people; it was just part of the job. He even grew accustomed to being shot at, which occurred on almost every mission.

He was on his second mission of the day, the first time they'd flown two missions in one day in more than two weeks. It was a reconnaissance run. They were looking for a downed Huey that had engine trouble and had been forced to land. Rick's crew was trying to get to them before the North Vietnamese Army (NVA) found them.

The downed chopper's radio was damaged, but it had been able to make a May Day call with its last coordinates just before it hit the ground. As Rick's crew traveled over the thick jungle, he could see a clearing just ahead. As they reached the opening, they could see that the field was covered with rice patties, with some solid ground around the perimeter. Off in the far corner of the field, they could see the downed helicopter sitting on the ground.

The crew looked to be engaged in a firefight with the NVA. As soon as they came within range of Rick's M60, the AC gave him the command to fire at will. Rick wasted no time spraying the NVA's position with a barrage of bullets. The door gunner's action drew the enemy's attention and they returned fire on the incoming Huey.

As they moved closer to the downed chopper, it appeared that there were only two surviving crew members. Rick's pilot was trying to get into position where he could come to a hover near the downed bird, so the survivors could jump in. But luck was not on the rescue ship's side. As they approached, Rick continued to fire, but he suddenly noticed that his right leg felt like he'd been stung by a hornet. He looked down at his leg and noticed the lower part of his pants leg just above his boot was now red. He'd been shot in his right calf, but he kept on firing.

Next the Huey's transmission was hit. Rick heard the grinding of the transmission as it began to seize up and the next thing he knew, he felt a thud as the Huey hit the ground.

Upon impact, Rick was knocked unconscious and was hanging upside down outside the helicopter, though still tethered by his monkey strap. Apparently, the combination of the crash landing and the bullet in his leg caused him to pass out cold. The rest of the crew members were okay, and the AC quickly radioed for help. Now there were two Hueys down. Fortunately, a third aircraft was nearby, but it was too risky for them to try to land and pick up the survivors. The downed crewmembers would have to hold off the enemy until the calvary arrived.

A few minutes later, a fourth bird came into view. It was able to provide suppressing fire while the third Huey landed and rescued the guys on the ground, including Rick.

Rick woke up in a field hospital. He had no recollection of what happened after his aircraft went down. But apparently, he was able to help fight off the NVA until they were rescued by the third chopper. He was officially classified as a WIA (Wounded in Action).

He'd suffered a concussion and the leg wound, but neither of them was severe. He remained in the hospital for a couple of weeks before returning to his unit.

Back in action, missions became fewer and fewer, mainly due to the American troop cutbacks. As 1972 ended, it was clear that the Americans were getting out of Vietnam. Rick's tour of Nam ended and in February, he was on his way back to the "world." By the end of March 1973, most U.S. troops were pulled out of Southeast Asia.

The fighting was now left up to the South Vietnamese Army. The South held out until the end of April 1975, when Saigon fell to the North Vietnamese, which for all practical purposes ended the war.

Rick served out the rest of his tour in the States and was honorably discharged at the end of 1973, returning to Chattanooga.

He was glad to be back home, but his life wasn't the same.

Chapter 4—Back Home

Rick was dressed in civilian clothes as he stepped off the bus at the Greyhound Bus station. He'd taken all of three steps when he was greeted by his mom, Lillie. She hugged him with all her might and tears of joy streamed down her face as she held on to him for several minutes. Her prayers had been answered. Rick had survived the war and had returned home safely, just in time to spend Christmas with her.

The two talked all the way home. Lillie pulled into the driveway and parked the car. Rick got out, opened the trunk, and lifted out his duffle bag. Then he opened the garage door and there sat his red Dodge Dart. He couldn't wait to take it out for a spin, but first he was hungry. His mom had prepared his favorite dinner—fried chicken, green beans, and mashed potatoes. She'd also made him a chocolate cake. Rick cleaned his plate and had a big piece of dessert. The two talked until almost midnight.

The next day after breakfast, he pulled the red Dodge out of the garage and was headed to UTC to register for the 1974 winter semester. Taking the long way, he drove down Brainerd Road and passed Shoney's, then took a right on East Brainerd Road. As he approached I-75, he took the westbound ramp toward downtown Chattanooga.

He looked back over his left shoulder and to his surprise, no cars were coming. He shifted into second gear and hit the gas. The red Dodge jumped forward. Rick wanted to see how fast he could get the car going before he reached the next mile marker. It was the same route where he'd raced many a car before Vietnam.

There were no cars in front of him as the engine kept winding, then he shifted into third and he was thrust back into his seat as the car jumped forward. When he hit the mile marker, the speedometer read 135 miles per hour. He eased off the gas and slowed down closer to the posted speed limit as he headed downtown. Rick still loved driving fast.

The next couple of weeks, he took it easy. On Christmas Eve, he went to church with his mother. She had a big smile on her face as they entered the sanctuary. Many welcomed Rick back home. The next day, they went to his grandmother's house for Christmas lunch.

At night when he went to bed, he often thought about his Army experience. In Vietnam, Rick had come to know the brutality of war. He had no idea how many men he'd killed, but it was a lot. He'd seen his buddies die in battle. Even though he hadn't been in battle for almost a year, the images of the blood, the guts, and the smell of death were still on his mind. Alcohol and drugs had helped him deal with the stress of battle and the boredom of waiting for the next mission.

A number of soldiers left Southeast Asia with a drug addiction. Fortunately for Rick, he wasn't one of them. He'd learned all about the different types of illegal drugs, from hallucinogens to the hard drugs like heroin. His own consumption, however, was limited to pot; occasionally, he smoked some hashish, but that was it. In the back of his mind, he thought that there was money to be made in selling drugs, but he wasn't sure it was the worth the risk.

It was 1974. The war in Vietnam was over for the Americans and Rick was ready to get back to a normal life. Classes at UTC started right after New Year's Day. On his first day back, he drove his red Dodge Dart down McCallie Avenue. He was looking forward to going back to school. For the moment, his wartime experiences were a distant memory. At school, Rick picked up where he left off before his journey was interrupted by the Army. He took a full course load and, thanks to the GI Bill, the government was paying for it.

As he settled back into school, his next goal was to find a place to live. He loved his mother, but at this stage of his life, he could no longer live at home. She was a teetotaler and Rick now had a fondness for beer and pot. He needed his freedom.

He soon started to reconnect with old friends. One of the first guys he found was Joe Dyer. Joe was three years older than Rick and they had gotten to know each other at the Rifle Club while Rick was still in high school. Joe wanted to know about Rick's experiences in combat and loved listening to him talk about his time in Southeast Asia. Dyer was fascinated when Rick described using the M60 machine gun as he mowed down the Viet Cong. Spencer gave him every gory detail. Unlike a lot of Vietnam vets, Rick didn't mind talking about his wartime experiences.

Joe started inviting Rick to parties, all of which included drugs. The parties allowed Rick to meet new friends and gain access to marijuana. He was introduced to a few of the local drug dealers. When asked about the war, Rick freely talked about his experiences. This slender, six-foot-one, 170-pound, shaggy-headed veteran was gaining the reputation of being a fun guy; most of his new friends also thought of him as a bad-ass, based on his Vietnam escapades. Rick was assimilating back into the civilian world in his hometown.

He still needed a place to live. He ran into two other old friends, Dave Prickett and Jim Lewis. Luckily for Rick, they were looking for a roommate and invited him to move in. Rick quickly accepted the offer and was soon living at 4700 Midland Pike. He wrote them a check for his share of the deposit and the first month's rent. Rick, being Rick, had plenty of money; he'd been saving almost all his pennies since the first day of Basic Training.

Rick settled into the school routine, but hadn't worked since he returned home. As February rolled around, his entrepreneurial spirit was itching and he was on the lookout for a job or a way of making money. While Rick was at war, the two carpet ladies had closed their business, so that wasn't an option. As he looked for employment, he started doing odd jobs for his mother's friends and neighbors.

He was still running into old friends. On a break between classes, he walked into the main canteen on campus and noticed me sitting by the window, drinking a Coke and reading a book. Rick, wearing his olive-green army jacket, walked over and without saying a word sat down. I looked up and was surprised to see Rick. I said, "What are you doing here?" I hadn't seen him since before he left for Vietnam.

Rick gave me the short version. We agreed that we needed to catch up. So we met the next day for a pizza at Shakey's on Brainerd Road.

It was around 7 p.m. and dark outside when I pulled into the restaurant's parking lot. I saw Rick's red Dodge Dart and knew he was already there. Cindy and I got out of my navy-blue Mustang and walked toward the restaurant. She also knew Rick from City High.

As we opened the door, we could smell pizza and cigarette smoke. The place had a decent crowd and there was the sound of muffled chatter from the various conversations going on at each table. Once inside, the restaurant was dark, even though there were windows in the front. The dark wood paneling that lined the walls, the dark wooden booths that circled the room, and the dimmed lights that sat on the tables all contributed to the dimness. In the center section of the room, a few people were seated around several wooden tables. Most of the customers were in the booths that surrounded the room. It took a few seconds for our eyes to adjust.

Rick was sitting in a booth on the right side of the restaurant with a pitcher of beer and the newspaper. He looked up and saw us approaching. He got up and gave Cindy a hug and we shook hands. We sat down and at once started chatting about old friends and what had been going on in Chattanooga while Rick was gone. We ordered a pizza and some more beer, then the conversation turned to Rick's time in Vietnam.

He held nothing back as he described his time riding shotgun as the door gunner on a Huey helicopter. He got excited talking about shooting "gooks" (otherwise known as Viet Cong) as they scurried about on the ground. From the look in his eyes, it was clear that he enjoyed it. Although she didn't say anything at the time, Rick scared Cindy with his stories and his descriptions of killing the "little bastards."

After his description about shooting gooks, he gave graphic accounts about his buddies getting killed and what it was like being shot at during the missions. He then went on to give the play-by-play of being shot in the leg, ending up in a rice patty, and waking up in the hospital.

After one large pizza and four pitchers of beer, Rick had finished his story. I'd talked to several Vietnam vets, but none were as graphic as Rick had been. We paid the check, walked outside, and said our goodbyes.

Once back in my Mustang, Cindy turned to me and exclaimed, "I don't want to be around him ever again! He's crazy! He liked killing people! He's not the same Rick!"

The Parties

About a month after the pizza dinner, I ran into Rick again at the canteen on campus. We talked for a while and Rick asked if I'd like to come to a party on Friday night. It was going to be at Rick's place on Midland Pike. Cindy was out of town, so I told him I'd be there. During college days in the '70s, parties were common and they weren't limited to weekends. If you wanted, you could find a party somewhere just about any day of the week.

I arrived at Rick's at about eight o'clock. When I pulled up in front, six or seven cars were already parked on the street in front of the small brick house, with another four or five in the driveway. I saw Rick's red Dodge Dart in the driveway and knew I was at the right place. I parked my Mustang on the street, got out, and walked toward the front door. I could hear music as I approached the house. Without knocking, I opened the front door and walked into a smoked-filled room. The smell of marijuana was dominant and Cream's "White Room" was playing on the stereo in the background.

Out of 20 or so people there, a few were girls, but it was mostly guys. Some were standing, some were seated, and a few already looked to be passed out or stoned out of their minds as they were sprawled out on the couch. Rick wasn't in the room and I asked where he was. One of the guys said he was in the back. I was then asked if I wanted a beer or joint. I chose a beer.

I wandered around the house and surprisingly, recognized only two or three people. This was unusual; I knew a lot of the same people Rick did, having gone to school together. I also noticed it was a drug cornucopia. Besides marijuana, I was offered the full gamut that included hash, quaaludes, cocaine, and a hit of acid. I even heard someone say something about shooting some heroin. I'd been to a lot of parties since I'd been in college, but I'd never seen anything like this. Pot, hash, and quaaludes were fairly common at parties in those days, but not hard drugs.

I was shocked at the variety and amount of dope. I didn't say anything about it, but I got scared, envisioning the next knock on the door from the narcotics squad, who would haul me and the rest of the bunch off to jail on multiple drug charges.

Rick showed up a few minutes later. He greeted me and introduced me to a few other guys as joints were passed around. After a little over an hour, I told Rick I was leaving, because I was meeting some other guys for a beer at JoJo's, a bar on Brainerd Road. The truth was I wanted to get the hell out of there.

It was the last time I was around Rick for that long. We still saw each other around campus or in town, but I was done with him. Cindy was right. He wasn't the same guy.

The "Gang"

The parties rotated from place to place. This was by design, so as not to draw too much attention to any one place. By spring, the parties were the core of Rick's social circle, where he met new people. Everyone who went to the parties was there to have a good time and drugs were a big part of the draw.

The attendees wore a blend of styles from the mid-'70s. Some were the stereotypical hippies with long hair, tie-dyed shirts, and bell-bottom jeans. Others looked like jocks or geeks, and some were a mixture of them all. It was a motley looking '70s group.

Rick had developed a core of friends that spent a lot of time together. They went to parties, the Rifle Club, and sometimes local bars, such as JoJo's or Leonard's. Rick's buddy Joe Dyer became a regular on the party scene. Rick also got to know Chip Grimes, one of Joe's friends, and the Logan brothers, John and Carl. It was an odd lot with different backgrounds and interests.

Joe P. Dyer III was the oldest. He had gone to East Ridge High School, where his interests were focused on theater and performing arts. He'd attended Highland Park Baptist Church most of his life and had been a Boy Scout in his younger days. He went to the University of Tennessee and was a semester away from receiving his Bachelor of Arts degree when he was kicked out of school for stealing a typewriter. In the spring of 1974, he moved back home with his parents and worked part-time at his father's bike shop.

Joe and Rick shared a love for guns, but Joe didn't just like to shoot, he also collected them and stored them in his parent's basement. He had a number of rifles that ranged from military to target. He also had an assortment of pistols, knives, and odds and ends, such as flares and a machine-gun barrel. Joe also had several thousand rounds of ammunition, including armor-piercing. It was quite a collection for a young man.

It took a while for Joe to get to know people and be comfortable around them. In general, he just didn't trust people. He also thought of himself as a tough guy and generally carried a pistol. He boasted that he wouldn't hesitate to use it if someone tried to rip him off.

Joe had become friends with Donald "Chip" Grimes Jr. after high school. Chip had graduated from Brainerd High School in 1970. In high school, he played in the marching band. After high school, he enrolled at Auburn University. His father had also gone to Auburn, where he'd played football. The senior Grimes was an executive in the carpet-machinery business. The family attended the Brainerd Presbyterian Church.

Chip also had a fondness for guns and sometimes went with Dyer to the Rifle Club. Chip didn't have an outgoing personality; he was quiet and rather reserved. I knew Chip Grimes; we both lived in Shepherd Hills, a neighborhood located on the side of Missionary Ridge. But we didn't run in the same circles.

The Logan brothers got to know the other guys at the parties. Both had gone to Notre Dame High School and been athletes. John had been a wrestler and was a fierce competitor on the mats. His outgoing personality allowed him to know everyone at school. He graduated in 1973.

Carl played football and had graduated with the class of 1974. Carl was the quieter of the two brothers. John and Carl lived together in an apartment in Brainerd. Carl hung out with the guys on occasion, but wasn't a regular.

John, on the other hand, spent a lot of time with Rick, Joe, and Chip. The four had become somewhat known as the "Pot and Gun Gang." Generally, if you saw one of them, you'd see the other three, unless Chip was away at school. The four bonded into a close-knit group, at least for a while.

Another young kid hung around the group from time to time. Steve Cannon had graduated from Brainerd High School in 1973. He frequented the parties and had become friends with Rick. His dad was a Navy man, so he had something in common with Rick, based on the military.

Guns and drugs had become the friendship thread among the young men. As the spring turned to summer, Rick used his entrepreneurial drive to start up a drug-dealing enterprise, his focus on selling pot. He knew his Vietnam reputation gave him an image as someone not to cross. It also allowed him to make the connections he needed to get into dealing. He'd learned all about drugs in Southeast Asia and he felt it was now time to get into the business.

The party circuit provided him with a customer base and his reputation gave him the security he needed. He'd also saved enough money to bankroll the venture.

He began selling marijuana, but he could source almost anything a customer wanted. It was a simple business, just buying and selling for cash. He sold most of his wares at the parties and the Pot and Gun Gang doubled as his de facto sales forces.

By the end of the summer, he was handling a lot of dope and cash, so he carried a gun with him most of the time. He favored his M1 carbine, which he generally left in the trunk of his car. He pulled it out only if he felt a threat or a need for protection.

Up to this point, the gang was just using and dealing marijuana, but the stakes would soon be raised.

The Drugstore Burglary

At the height of the summer of 1974, Rick's drug business grew. He'd become a reliable source for marijuana in the Brainerd area of town. But unbeknownst to him, he'd also gotten the attention of the narcotics detectives. He was now on their radar.

It was a hot summer afternoon, almost dusk, as shotgun blasts echoed across the range. The Chattanooga Rifle Club had a number of ranges for all types of guns. Places to shoot a variety of guns ranged from pistols and hunting rifles to shotguns. The gang had the range to themselves as they blasted clay pigeons out of the air, but it was time to quit; it was almost too dark to see the flying yellow and black clays. The men cleaned up their shotguns, stored them away in their cases, sat down at a picnic table, and fired up a joint.

Chip Grimes had recently come back from Auburn and told the others he'd gotten into trouble in Alabama. He didn't want his father to know about it, so he needed some money to hire a lawyer. The guys kicked around some ideas, but nothing seemed to make sense. Then someone said, "Maybe you should just rob a bank."

Rick chimed in, "How about a drug store?"

"What good would that do?" one replied.

Spencer retorted, "Well, obviously, they have some drugs, but they also have money orders, which are just as good as cash."

After a moment of silence, Joe asked how that would work.

Since Rick had worked at Drew's Drugs in Dalewood for many years while he was going to school, he knew the store layout well. He said, "The money orders are in a metal box under the pharmacy counter."

Then Joe asked about the drugs.

"The narcotics are locked up in a safe, but some diet pills are on the shelves behind the pharmacy counter."

Grimes was also familiar with the store. His family had shopped there for years.

By now it was pitch black and they left the rifle range. Rick was the last one out, so he stopped his Dodge on the gravel driveway, got out, closed the chain-link gate, and locked the padlock. He got back in the Dodge, took a right on Hunter Road, and headed to Midland Pike.

A few days later there was big national news: Richard Nixon became the first U.S. president to resign from office, due to the fallout from the Watergate scandal. He was succeeded by Vice President Gerald Ford. The man responsible for getting American troops out of Vietnam was now out of office.

The gang reconvened at Rick's place a couple of days after their last gathering at the Rifle Club. Joe Dyer wanted to talk further about the possible drugstore caper. Dyer and Grimes had been talking about it and liked the idea. The next question was how they'd break in. They discussed various options, then Rick said, "Just knock a hole in the back wall."

The others looked at him like he was crazy.

"A few years ago, I was working there when a delivery truck backed into the back wall and almost came into the store. It was quickly repaired. The back wall is made of cinderblocks, hollow in the middle. You could take a sledgehammer and in a matter of minutes knock a hole in the wall big enough to crawl through. If the checks are still in the same place, you could grab them and the pills and be out of there in less than five minutes."

Joe and Chip grinned at each other and Joe said, "Let's go take a look at the store."

It was about 11:30 p.m. They all jumped in Joe's car and headed over to the drugstore to check out the layout and look at the back wall. There was an Esso gas station on the corner of Wilcox Boulevard and Shallowford Road and behind it sat a strip shopping center with Drew's Drugs, a toy store, and the Red Food grocery store. They drove around back and stopped behind the painted block wall of the drug store. A dumpster blocked the view from cars coming down Shallowford Road.

They could see only one problem.

The drug store closed at nine p.m., but the grocery store closed at 11. A couple of days a week, the Red Food store received shipments after midnight and sometimes the stocking boys worked the midnight shift resupplying the shelves. The gang would need to find a time when Red Food wasn't stocking late at night.

When they got back to Rick's place, he told them that he wouldn't be involved in the drugstore heist. First, he didn't need the money and second, he might become an easy suspect, since he'd worked there. He was also concerned that his drug business was getting some attention from the narc squad and he wanted to keep a low profile.

Logan, Grimes, and Dyer understood his reasoning, but they were all in on the scheme. It sounded like an easy score. The next step was to find the right time.

The trio observed the drug and grocery stores at night for a couple of weeks. They noticed that no one was working around

Red Food on Sunday nights. So, they picked the Sunday night before Labor Day to do the break-in. The drug store would be closed on Labor Day and most likely it would be Tuesday morning before the robbery was discovered.

It was a dark night with only a small sliver of moonlight illuminating the area. Just after midnight in the early morning of September 2, 1974, the three men arrived at the drug store. They drove into the shopping center's parking lot from the Shallowford Road entrance. The car rolled slowly in front of the toy store, then by the drug store, and lastly the grocery store. The parking lot wrapped around the stores until it hit an alley that ran behind the complex.

As they passed Red Food, the car slowly turned left with the lights turned off. The car moved in the darkness along the parking lot down along the side of the building and turned left into the alleyway. The long building was on the left and houses sat to the right, separated from the strip center by a row of bushes and trees.

They pulled up near the dumpster behind the drug store and stopped the car, but kept the engine running in case they needed to make a quick getaway. The three men, all dressed in dark clothes, got out of the car and opened the trunk. They pulled out two sledgehammers and a bag containing various tools. The heads of the big mallets had been wrapped with cloth towels to somewhat muffle the sound as they struck the cinderblock walls.

Dyer and Logan would be doing the heavy work with sledges. Grimes was designated as the lookout. He was holding a small walkie talkie and was stationed next to the dumpster. Dyer also had one, which he'd carry inside the store. It was a way to communicate if Grimes saw trouble. No cars were coming up or down the road. The coast was clear. The hammer crew put on gloves and stocking caps, then went to work.

Luckily, it was a cool night for this time of year, with the temperatures in the low 70s.

Thanks to their planning, they knew exactly where to start the hole. It took them only five minutes to make it big enough to crawl through. As Dyer and Logan disappeared into the store, Grimes placed the hammers and the tool bag back in the trunk. The intruders each carried a pair of wire-cutting pliers, a screwdriver, and a carpenter's hammer, in case they needed to break into a cabinet or cupboard. Both also had a pillowcase to load up their treasures.

Based on Spencer's description of the pharmacy's layout and their own observations as customers over the past few weeks, they knew exactly where to go. The checks were under the counter as Rick had described and the pills were on the shelves behind the cash register. In less than three minutes, the thieves got what they came for and were on their bellies crawling out of the hole. Once outside they threw the pillowcases and tools in the trunk and took off. They turned on the car's headlights and slowly drove out of the parking lot, then turned right onto Shallowford Road. They headed to Logan's place and could hardly wait to get there to see the size of the haul.

Now What?

It was late afternoon on Labor Day and the three headed over to Spencer's place. When Dyer, Grimes, and Logan arrived, Spencer and his roommates were watching TV. Once inside the apartment Dyer announced, "We did it! We got away with it!"

Rick asked, "Well, what did you get?"

"About five thousand pills, a mix of uppers and downers. We also got a handful of cashier's checks."

The trio was excited and proud of their accomplishment and gave Rick a detailed account of their work.

So far, there had been nothing on the news about the break-in. Spencer said, "Nobody will know about it until tomorrow morning at seven when the store manager opens up, unless someone drives by, sees the hole in the wall, and reports it."

The inevitable next question was, "Now what?"

Spencer suggested that they don't do anything for a least the next 30 days, lest they draw attention. "By then, things should be cooled off enough that you can sell the pills and start writing checks."

Everyone agreed.

The three then asked Rick if he could get rid of the pills for them.

"It will take some time to move that many pills, but I'll see what I can do. Not until October, though, when they won't be so hot. Until then, I'll hide them in a safe place."

Dyer, Logan, and Grimes had committed to pay Spencer a 40% commission for everything he sold and the three would split the balance equally. Once again, there was complete agreement with the plan and the timetable.

As far as the checks went, Dyer would put them in a watertight box and hide them at the Rifle Club. When they started cashing them, whoever cashed them would get to keep 50% of the value and the other two would get 25% each. They all thought that was fair, because cashing the checks was the risky part of the deal.

Chip Grimes returned to school at Auburn and planned to be back in mid-October. Logan and Dyer returned to their daily routines and kept a low profile.

Surprisingly, the drug-store break-in never made the news, most likely because the Drew's Drugs management didn't want the publicity. The customers knew something had happened as the neighborhood chatter got around and it was easy to see the construction work going on to repair the hole in the wall. Regardless of the news or lack thereof, the Chattanooga police were working on the case and had been interviewing employees and people who were connected to the store. The police didn't contact Spencer, since it had been over three years since he worked there.

A few days later, Dyer dropped off the pills at Spencer's place. Rick packed them in a couple of plastic bags and hid some in the woods on Missionary Ridge and the rest at the Rifle Club. He'd used these places before to hide drugs and felt comfortable that they were safe.

The last week of September, Joe Dyer called Spencer wanting to know if he'd sold any pills.

"I told you, Joe, I'm not touching them until October."

Dyer replied, "Yeah, I know, but I want my money."

"Well, you're just going to have to wait!"

The first week of October, Spencer retrieved the smaller of the two hidden packages from the Rifle Club. He managed to sell them all in just a few days. The bulk of the haul or about two-thirds of the pills were stashed on the Ridge.

The next night, it was dark when he went to retrieve them. He'd hidden the pills in the woods on the north side of South Crest Road behind the Ohio Civil War Monument. Rick parked his car, got out, and with a flashlight in hand walked past the large monument. He entered the woods where he picked up a walking trail. It led down the hill toward the McCallie School at the base of the ridge. About 100 yards in, he turned on the flashlight. At that point, he'd reached a large oak tree where he veered off the trail to the right.

He walked about 20 yards through the thick woods before reaching a sizable pine tree that had been struck by lightning. The tree was still upright, but the bark had been knocked off on one side and a split in the trunk ran from top to bottom. At the base of the tree was a large flat rock, which had been covered by recently fallen leaves. Rick stopped here, brushed off the leaves with his foot, and bent down to pick up the rock. He moved the rock and shined his light into a hole about a foot square and six inches deep.

There was nothing in the hole.

Rick was stunned.

He'd stashed the pills here just over three weeks earlier. He shone his light around the base of the tree, but saw nothing. The pills were gone.

He replaced the rock and decided to come back the next day and look again in the daylight. He wanted to make sure he hadn't missed something in the dark. He turned off his flashlight and walked back up the hill, running through the various scenarios as to what could have happened to the stash.

By mid-morning, he was back at the monument and retracing his steps from the night before. He searched all around, but the pills were simply not there. He could only assume someone had found and taken them. He had no choice but to tell Dyer and the others what happened.

Spencer didn't waste any time and met with Dyer to tell him about the missing pills. Dyer demanded $1,000 for the lost drugs, but Rick said he wasn't going to pay, because that was just part of the risk when it came to selling drugs.

An intense argument ensued between the two. Dyer left the meeting and said, "This issue is not over!"

Over the next couple of days, Rick mentally retraced his steps on the day he hid the drugs on Missionary Ridge, but he didn't come up with anything new. The lost pills were never found.

A few days later, Dyer went to Spencer's place again, where Rick was talking to his friend Steve Lawson. Dyer joined the conversation and after a few minutes, Joe and Rick moved to

Spencer's bedroom for a private discussion. They were in there for a while and when they returned, Dyer said, "We'll settle this at a later date."

Rick simply replied, "Okay," and Dyer left.

Hearing this, Lawson wasn't sure what it meant.

The Last Deal

Rick had grown weary of the drug business. He was making good money, but he wasn't sure it was worth the hassle. He was also fearful that the police were on to him and it was just a matter of time before they popped him. Then there were the lost pills and the conflict with his friend Joe. All the issues made him seriously consider getting out of the drug business.

The week of October 7, Rick had another meeting with Dyer. This time Joe told Spencer that he had a marijuana deal for him. A guy by the name of John Fry would sell Rick up to 10 pounds of pot. He could buy it for $100 a pound, a very attractive price. Fry had gone to school with Logan and would be in town sometime next week. Rick told Dyer to let him know and he'd be glad to meet Fry. Dyer told him that he'd pass on the message and would be there to make the introduction. Rick was okay with that.

Spencer was surprised that Dyer hadn't mentioned the lost pills again.

While Dyer was playing nice with Rick, he told John Logan that he felt Spencer had ripped him off over the pills. "And when someone rips off Joe Dyer, there are three things I can do to balance the scales—not associate with him, take something from him, or take care of him."

The last comment sent shivers up Logan's spine.

Next, Dyer told Logan about his conversation with Spencer and about the drug deal with John Fry.

Logan asked, "How do you know Fry?"

Dyer replied, "I don't, but you do, and Spencer has probably heard of him and knows he's a drug dealer."

Logan asked, "What's the point of a fake drug deal?"

Joe Dyer looked him in the eye and said, "That's how we get our money back!"

On the night of October 15, Grimes called Dyer from Auburn and told him he'd be in town the next day. He needed some money for his legal problems in Alabama. The next afternoon, Chip arrived in Chattanooga and rode with Dyer and Logan to the Rifle Club to retrieve the stolen money orders.

The checks had been wrapped in plastic and stored in a small metal box that had been hidden in the woods 50 yards from the entrance, just off the gravel driveway. They retrieved the box and headed back to Logan's apartment in Brainerd. The checks were dry and looked new. It would be easy to pass them off. All they needed was a check-writing machine.

That night they celebrated Chip's return home with a small party at a friend's house. The next morning, October 17, the three went downtown to Meyer Business Machines on Market Street and bought a check embosser. The machine would print the amount on the blank checks and make them look legitimate. Most businesses would accept these cashier's checks without asking questions.

With the money-making machine in hand, the three returned to Logan's apartment and Grimes began running money orders through the check embosser. He was virtually printing money. Once he cashed them, he would have enough money to pay off the lawyer in Alabama.

Around four p.m., Grimes finished printing checks. At this point, Dyer asked Logan to join them in the kitchen, where he outlined his plan for the night. He told them about the fake drug deal with John Fry that he'd told Spencer about last week. He continued, "We go over to Rick's and tell him the deal is on. Then we head to the Rifle Club and Rick meets us there. Once he gets there, we gather at the fire pit in the woods, sit down, and talk. Rick will have the cash on him to pay Fry for the pot. We pretend that we're waiting on Fry to show up. After about thirty minutes or so, Rick will be tired of waiting and will get up. This is when we pull out our guns and demand our money."

Dyer went into the other room and asked John's brother Carl for his pistol, a .45 semi-automatic. Carl gave it to him. Dyer unloaded the rounds in the gun, replaced them with his own ammunition, and handed it to Chip Grimes. "Let's go get our money back!"

After hearing the plan, John Logan was reluctant to go, but Dyer insisted. Carl Logan remained at the apartment. He was expecting friends to come over and watch TV. As they left the apartment, Chip Grimes had the .45, John Logan had a 9mm, and Joe Dyer was armed with a shotgun.

The three drove over to Spencer's apartment. They pulled into the driveway and Rick came outside to talk to them. Joe told Rick that the drug deal was on. John Fry was supposed to meet the gang with the pot at the Rifle Club.

Rick said, "Okay, we're on our way."

Spencer walked back inside to retrieve his M1 carbine, $1,400 in cash, and his friend Steve Cannon. Steve's dad had dropped him off at Spencer's earlier in the afternoon. Cannon was going with Rick to watch his back. Spencer always liked to take someone with him on a big deal for added security. He put on his jean jacket; it was beginning to get cool outside, and the temperatures were supposed to drop into the 40s during the night.

52

As Rick and Cannon were heading out the door, Steve Lawson said, "Are you sure you want to do this? Dyer still thinks you owe him a grand. This deal sounds kind of like a set-up to me."

Rick replied, "I'll have to take my chances and if I don't come back, you'll know who did it and you can go after them. Anyway, I told you this would be my last deal. After we sell this load, the only thing I'll be doing with pot is smoking it. We've got to get going, because after the deal is done, we're going over to Cannon's house for dinner. See you later."

Later that night, around 10:30, Dyer called Spencer's apartment. Dave Pricket answered the phone and Joe asked to speak with Rick.

Dave said, "He isn't here. I haven't seen him since earlier this afternoon. I thought he was supposed to meet up with you."

Dyer replied, "He was, but he didn't show up."

As Dave hung up the phone, he said to himself, "Something fishy is going on."

Over in East Ridge, Spencer and Cannon never showed up for dinner and Jim Cannon, Steve's father, began to worry about his son.

Chapter 5—The Men Are Missing

When they woke up, Rick's roommates didn't think much about Rick not being there. He could have crashed somewhere after a night of partying or he could have hooked up with a girl. But things began to change around mid-morning when Steve Cannon's father called and asked if Steve was there. He wasn't. Then he asked to talk to Rick.

"Rick didn't come home last night."

There was silence on the other end of the phone. Then Mr. Cannon said, "Well, if Steve or Rick show up, have them call me. Thanks."

Dave Prickett and Jimmy Lewis looked at each other. They didn't say anything, but they knew something was seriously wrong.

Jim Cannon had been making calls to Steve's friends all morning with no luck, so he decided to start looking for him. He got in his car and drove to places he knew Steve liked to go. He first went to the backside of Lookout Mountain. They'd camped there and he knew Steve liked to hike through the woods. By the time he finished his search, it was dark. He'd had no luck locating his son.

The next morning, the senior Cannon continued his search. First, he went to a farm in Ringgold that Steve had visited many times, then he drove to the Chattanooga Rifle Club on Hunter Road. Again, no luck. He concluded that his son had disappeared without a trace and he notified the police.

Rumors began to circulate around the party scene that Spencer had fled town, because the cops were on to him about selling pot. It was a believable story, but Rick's roommates didn't buy it. They knew Rick would have told them if he had to flee. Furthermore, they remembered what Steve Lawson had told them the night Rick left to meet the drug dealer and the Pot and Gun Gang. Spencer's words were, "If I don't come back, you'll know who did it." Based on this, Prickett and Lewis paid a visit to Dyer and Logan. They wanted to confront them face to face and see their reaction.

The roommates drove over the Logan's apartment and Dyer was there. When asked about Spencer and Cannon, they both denied any knowledge of their whereabouts. Dyer claimed that Spencer and Cannon didn't show up at the Rifle Club on the appointed night. It was a brief conversation and neither of the roommates believed Logan's or Dyer's story. They knew they had to be involved.

By the end of the weekend, the police were starting to make inquiries about Spencer and Cannon. Rick's mother Lillie Spencer was in Paris working for Greater European Mission. She routinely called Rick on Sunday nights and Rick always made a point to be there, since it was an international call. On Sunday October 20, she called as usual, but this time she was shocked by the response. The roommate who answered the phone told her that Rick wasn't there and they hadn't seen him in couple of days. The roommate also told her that the police were looking for him.

She hung up in a state of shock. After she collected her thoughts, she called the Chattanooga Police Department. Fortunately, she talked with someone who knew something about the case. The officer couldn't tell her anything she didn't already know, which wasn't much, but she'd at least confirmed her son was missing. The question in her mind was, "Where's Rick?" Her next call was to Air France. She was going back to Tennessee as soon as she could get a flight.

Searching for Clues

Lillie Spencer arrived back in Chattanooga and her first stop was the Police Department.

She walked in the entrance and was tired, but didn't look it. She wore a knee-length overcoat; her dark black hair was neatly kept and she was wearing black horn-rimmed glasses.

The chief detective told her they still didn't know much more than they did the last time the department had talked to her. He told her about the list of people they'd talked to and they gave her another shocking bit of news: Rick had been under surveillance for some time for selling drugs. She didn't say a word, just stared at the detective. She thought, "It can't be true. I raised him to know better than that!"

As she drove home, the shock about Rick's involvement in drugs was beginning to wear off. She knew he hadn't been the same since he returned from Vietnam. The news broke her heart, but she accepted it and the more she thought about it, the more she was convinced that the drugs were somehow related to his disappearance.

It had been almost a week since the men disappeared. There hadn't been a trace of them or Rick's car. According to the local gossip, the two had skipped town. But that all changed when the police got the first real clue in the case.

On October 24, a week after Rick had last been seen, a motorist stopped on the side of Interstate 24 near the Germantown Road exit with car trouble. There, he found a wallet, which he turned over to the Chattanooga police. It was Rick's. It still had his driver's license and credit cards, but no cash.

The police continued to follow up on leads. They talked to the roommates, Steve Lawson, and Logan and Dyer. In the meantime, Lillie Spencer had been making more calls to Rick's friends and associates, but there was still no sign of Rick or Steve.

Five days later, another clue turned up.

On the morning of Tuesday, October 29, a manager at the Eastgate Shopping Center called the police and told them about a red car in the parking lot that had been there for over a week. A police officer met the manager, who pointed out the car, parked on the far side of the large parking lot, near the golf course.

The officer pulled up behind the red car, radioed the tag number to headquarters, and asked them to run the plates to see who the car was registered to. He knew it would take a few minutes for a response. As he waited, he got out of the squad car and walked around the red 1971 Dodge Dart. He thought it was rather odd that the front windows were rolled down and the keys were in the ignition.

A few minutes later, the dispatcher radioed back that the car was registered to Roderick Cason Spencer, then instructed him not to touch anything and stay with the car until the detectives arrived. Twenty minutes later the two detectives, dressed in coats and ties, arrived. Shortly thereafter, a flatbed tow truck rolled up next to the red car. The investigators talked to the uniformed officer for a few minutes, put on gloves, and began to look inside the car. After a few minutes, they retrieved the keys and walked to the back of the car and opened the trunk. The truck was empty except for a spare tire and a jack. They were hoping to find a clue, maybe Spencer's M1 carbine, drugs, or money, but no luck.

The search continued for another 15 minutes. Then the car was hoisted up on the flatbed and taken to the police garage where it was dusted for fingerprints and checked for any evidence that might be helpful in the investigation.

Rick's car had been found, but where were the young men?

The Trail Goes Cold

On November 1, 1974, two weeks since the two men had last been seen, the final inspection report of the '71 Dodge was made available. The inspection didn't provide any usable information, except that red mud was found on the tires and underbelly. The Dodge had been off the road somewhere, but where?

One of the detectives thought that the red mud might be the key to the whereabouts of the two. Another said, "You might be right, but there's a lot of red clay in eastern Tennessee and north Georgia, so that's not a huge help."

The party-circuit gossip had now gone from Spencer and Cannon being out of town to their being dead. People who knew Rick were convinced that he wouldn't abandon his beloved Dodge Dart.

By mid-November, however, the police had exhausted most of their leads. It had been a month since the two young men had gone missing and the police had talked to everyone they could find who had any knowledge of them. Lillie Spencer and the Cannons still held out hope, but had lost confidence in the local police and began to look elsewhere for help.

They appealed to the District Attorney, Gary Gerbitz, to step up the effort. He saw their frustration with the case and called on the Tennessee Bureau of Investigation (TBI) for help. By now, the Hamilton County Sheriff's Department had also stepped up their efforts. The U.S. Treasury Department's Bureau of Alcohol, Tobacco, and Firearms was now aiding in the search, since drugs were suspected to be involved.

Law enforcement represented by city, county, state, and federal personnel launched renewed efforts with an all-out search beginning on Saturday, November 23. As new investigators joined the team, more questions were asked about who the logical suspects in the disappearance of the two young men might be. Thanks to the help of the new sets of eyes reviewing the information, the most plausible answer was the Pot and Gun Gang. But the accelerated effort didn't stop there.

The unified law-enforcement team hit the ground running and it was obvious. Tennessee Highway Patrol helicopters flew all over the county. Jeeps covered old dirt roads from Raccoon Mountain to Soddy Daisy. A fleet of small boats searched the waterways from Chickamauga Creek to the Tennessee River to Chickamauga Lake. Finally, an intense effort was underway to find the pair.

The effort brought out the news reporters and local TV stations to cover the massive search. The public was asked to let the local authorities know if they knew anything about the missing young men. Sure enough, information about the pair's disappearance started to come in and by Wednesday afternoon, law enforcement got the tip they needed.

The Search Leads to the Club

November 27 was a cool Wednesday afternoon and based on the credible leads the police had received, all roads led to the Chattanooga Rifle Club. The Pot and Gun Gang's names were also frequently mentioned and investigators talked again to Joe Dyer, John Logan, and Chip Grimes. Grimes was still away at school, but he'd be back in town soon, since it was close to Thanksgiving. So they started with Dyer and Logan.

Both admitted they'd been to the Rifle Club with Spencer a number of times, but denied any knowledge of Rick's or Cannon's disappearance. They did, however, admit that they were to meet Spencer at the Rifle Club in the early evening of October 17 for a drug deal, but that Spencer never showed up.

While Dyer and Logan were being questioned, a team of detectives, agents, and inspectors were at the Rifle Club to search the grounds. The detectives asked the two if they would ride to the Club and show them where they'd waited for Spencer. Both agreed.

It was late afternoon, but still daylight, when they headed to the Club. There wasn't a lot of talk as the car eased onto I-75 heading east. They only traveled about a mile when they exited on State Road 153 toward the Chickamauga Dam. Then they drove a few miles before turning off on Highway 58 heading east. Every once and a while, one of the detectives asked a random question, which received a short reply.

As they headed east, Logan just stared out the window, remembering the last time he traveled on this road. It was on that fateful night in October.

After about seven miles, Chickamauga Lake came into view on the left side of the road and a moment later, the car turned right onto Hunter Road. Two miles down the road they came to the Chattanooga Rifle Club sign and the car turned left onto the gravel driveway that led up a small hill.

At the top of the hill, a chain-link fence enclosed the property. The gate that straddled the driveway was opened and the detectives drove onto the property, staying on the gravel drive that ran beside a small meadow to the left. They followed the drive until it stopped in the parking lot, where six or seven other law-enforcement vehicles were parked.

The Club was founded in 1927 and had been in this location since 1958. The property covered 20-plus acres. The gravel and red-clay parking lot was surrounded by a number of different types of shooting ranges, such as high-powered rifle, pistol, skeet shooting, and several special target ranges. Most of the ranges were built in a semicircle layout into the side of small hills that surrounded most of the property.

As they exited the cars, Logan appeared to be nervous, though Dyer was cool as a cucumber and showed no emotion. Detectives asked the young men about the night they were supposed to meet Spencer. They pointed out where they parked and where they waited for Rick, in the woods to the left of the parking lot.

They led the detectives over to a small clearing in the woods about 50 feet from the parking lot. In the middle of the opening, a circle of rocks enclosed an old campfire. By then, it had gotten dark, and the temperature was beginning to drop. By midnight, it was forecasted to be in the 20s. Dyer and Logan were wearing light jackets and starting to get cold.

The woods were being searched by 10-12 officers All were armed with flashlights as they looked for clues and bodies. As they moved through the woods, their lights bounced around among the trees and it looked like a swarm of giant fireflies flying in a zig-zag pattern.

The detectives wanted to hear the story about that night again.

"We got here around five-thirty and parked the car. We walked into the woods and gathered around this fire pit."

"Who's 'we'?"

"The two of us and Chip Grimes."

"Where's Grimes?"

"Still at Auburn. We haven't talked to him lately."

"What did you do once you got to the clearing?"

"We built a fire, sat down, and waited. We waited 'til about seven-thirty, then left. It didn't look like Spencer or Fry was going to show up. We went to get something to eat."

Then Dyer added, "When we got back to Logan's, I was concerned about Rick and called his apartment to see if he was there. I was told he wasn't."

The investigator then asked, "Who's Fry?"

Dyer replied, "He's the guy who was going to sell Spencer the pot."

The question-and-answer session went on for another 10 minutes, then it was interrupted.

City Narcotics Detective Joe McCullough had been slowly walking through the woods shining his flashlight on the ground. Suddenly, the light reflected off a object in the leaves. He bent down and discovered it was a small metal button on a jean jacket. He pulled the jacket out of the leaves and saw a couple of holes in it and what appeared to be bloodstains. The detective continued to dig through the leaves and uncovered a bloodstained T-shirt, a pair of blue jeans, a belt, and a pair of tennis shoes. He assumed these had belonged to one of the men and that meant the bodies must be nearby.

McCullough continued cautiously. About fifty yards from where he'd found the clothes, he tripped over something. He wasn't sure what it was, but he knew it wasn't a stick or a rock. He reached down under the leaves to feel it and when he touched it, he knew what it was. It was flesh. He gently brushed the leaves away and sure enough, it was an arm. He'd found the grave!

The detective yelled out, "Hey, I think I've found something over here!"

Chapter 6—A Grizzly Discovery

The bodies were found about 100 yards northwest from the front gate. Several of the nearby officers rushed over to see what had been found. The detective quizzing Dyer and Logan stayed with them in the clearing.

McCullough gave instructions to the others as they arrived. "We have a crime scene here, so let's be careful! Let's get some lights over here, stake off the area, and clear the ground around the grave. Sift through the leaves *carefully* as you clear them away. We might find some more clues. Somebody get a couple of shovels and a few tarps. I want the dirt from the grave on one tarp. We may want to give it a thorough going over tomorrow in the daylight. I want the body on another one."

Once the portable lights were placed around the grave and turned on, it was as bright as daylight. The leaves were cleared and it was easy to see the outline of a makeshift grave, plus the arm that was exposed from elbow to hand.

As the digging began, Sheriff Frank Newell radioed a request for an ambulance and the mobile crime lab. The grave was so shallow that detectives were on their hands and knees, cautiously digging around the body, trying not to do further damage to the remains. After a few minutes of digging, they discovered not one body, but two, in the shallow grave, less than two feet deep, the bodies stacked one on top of the other. Both were badly decomposed and no form of identification was found in the grave. But there was little doubt in any of the investigators' minds that they were the bodies of Spencer and Cannon.

As the bodies were placed on the tarp, the detectives could see that both corpses had been shot in the head and a few times in their upper body. It had been a brutal killing and most of the investigators commented that they'd never seen anything like it. But one thing seemed odd to the investigators. The two were wearing only their underwear and socks.

As the bodies were removed from the shallow grave, Logan and Dyer were escorted over to the burial site. As the bodies came within view of the two, Logan went to pieces, wailing as he fell to the ground and throwing up, while Dyer showed no emotion.

Soon thereafter, the Tri Community ambulance arrived.

Next, the city's mobile crime lab came rumbling up the Rifle Club's gravel driveway. It looked like a refitted Winnebago and had "Chattanooga Police Department" in bold lettering on each side. The large vehicle would be used as a mobile command post on the scene until the investigation was complete.

After a short meeting among the lead investigators, the two dead men were put in body bags, placed in the ambulance, and taken to Erlanger Hospital in Chattanooga, where the autopsies would be performed.

Meanwhile, the press had also arrived, but they were given limited access to the murder site. They were allowed to take photos of the bodies being loaded into the ambulance and the activity in the parking lot, but were kept out of the woods. The reporters were told that a statement would be made in the morning.

A small army of law-enforcement personnel still armed with flashlights were scurrying about the grounds looking for any additional evidence that could help them identify the killer or killers. While all this was going on, Dyer and Logan walked back to the campfire in the clearing with the detective who'd been with them since they'd arrived.

He continued the questioning for another 15 minutes, then finally said, "I have one last question. Did you boys have anything to do with the murders?"

Both gave a quick reply. "No!"

After a moment of silence, the detective said, "Okay, let's get in the car and we'll take you home."

Dyer and Logan walked out of the woods with the detective and got in the back seat of the police car. The two detectives who rode out with them were in the front seat.

As the car pulled out of the gravel driveway onto Hunter Road, Dyer muttered to himself, "We didn't mean for it to go this far."

One of the detectives asked him, "What did you say?"

"Nothing, but whoever killed Spencer and Cannon ought to get the electric chair."

From that point on, nothing was said the rest of the way back to Logan's apartment. As they got out of the car, the driver said, "Thanks for your help. I'm sure we'll have some more questions for you later, so stay around town."

"Yes sir."

Once the detective's car was out of site, Logan looked at Dyer and said, "What do we do now?"

"Nothing. Just keep your cool. They don't have anything that connects us to the murders."

Dyer got in his car and drove off, while Logan walked into his apartment. He sat in a chair and started sobbing. He looked at his brother and said, "What am I going to do?"

John gave his brother Carl all the details about his afternoon with the police.

Carl said, "You have two options. Tell the police what you know or say nothing!"

John put his face in his hands and continued crying, thinking, "What am I going to do?"

Thanksgiving Day

The day after the bodies were discovered was November 28, Thanksgiving Day. It was anything but the normal day of celebration with families and friends for the Spencer and the Cannon families. Instead, they were grieving and planning funerals.

It was no holiday either for law enforcement, medical examiners, and news media as they all looked for more answers in the Rifle Club murders. The detectives continued walking the grounds out at the Club. The medical examiners worked on the badly decomposed bodies and the news media started putting the story together. At Erlanger Hospital, the autopsies had been performed and the bodies were identified. The heads of the various law-enforcement agencies involved in the investigation were summoned to the morgue for a briefing on the findings.

Once they were all there, the coroner gave them the report. As expected, the bodies were those of Rick Spencer, age 21, and 18-year-old Steve Cannon. They'd been positively identified by their dentists who compared their dental records to the remains.

The autopsies revealed that Spencer had been shot with a shotgun, once in the head, a blast so powerful that the entire back half of his skull was missing. There was no doubt that it was a close-range shot. He'd also been shot three other times—once in the right arm, once in the left arm, and once in the left side. Multiple double-aught buckshot pellets were found in his torso.

Cannon was also shot with a shotgun, in the head at close range, as the entire right side of his face and skull had been blown away. Cannon also had a two-inch hole in the left side of his chest and buckshot was found in his chest and abdomen.

It was clear that a shotgun had been used as the murder weapon for both young men, except Cannon also had a .45 bullet wound in his back between the shoulder blades. That wound raised more questions and with this information, investigators surmised that there must have been two shooters.

Now that the bodies had been identified, the detectives were given the onerous task of telling the young men's parents. As expected, Lillie Spencer and the Cannons were devastated with the news. The anxiety of not knowing their sons' whereabouts was over, but the emotions were now flipped to dealing with life without their sons. The only questions that remained were who did it and why, which the many law enforcement agencies were diligently working on.

The Press Conference

Since the parents had been notified of their sons' demise, a press conference was called to update the media. Various officials gave reports. The dead men were identified, along with graphic descriptions of their wounds. Authorities believed that the pair had been ambushed and the motive was most likely a robbery involving drugs and money.

TBI agent Joe Hannah addressed the gathering. "I want to highly compliment the news media for helping us by publicizing the search. We might not have received the tip we needed to find the bodies without their help."

The gathered media heard that the investigation was ongoing. The law-enforcement team consisted of local, state, and federal personnel who would continue working until the murderer or murderers were found. The authorities hoped to make a quick arrest.

Local TV stations and newspapers immediately reported the information. The story of finding the missing men became the talk around Thanksgiving tables in Chattanooga. Turkey dinners and football took a backseat.

While the news hit the airways, law enforcement kept looking for clues. As most local citizens sat down to eat their dinners, investigators continued to search the Rifle Club. Spencer's clothes had been found the night before, but further inspection of the garments revealed that they'd been removed after he was shot. The holes in the shirt and jacket matched the wounds found on his body, all confirmed by the autopsy.

Since Cannon was found in his underwear, his clothes must be in the woods somewhere as well. Investigators were also combing the grounds looking for the murder weapons, along with Spencer's M1 carbine, money, and drugs. They used metal detectors to cover the wooded area and found several spent shotgun shells, which were collected for evidence. They would be tested to see if they matched the pellets that were found in the bodies.

Cannon had been seen wearing an orange T-shirt. Around mid-morning, that was found in another section of the woods. It had two large holes in it caused by the shotgun blast. From the looks of it, he must have been shot at close range due to the powder burns.

At one time, the site of the Rifle Club had been a farm with a house and several other outbuildings. The original buildings were long gone and the only remains of the homestead were a circular stone cistern. It had been used to collect drinking water. A two-foot-high stone wall protected the five-foot-diameter hole that was estimated to be about 20 feet deep and was half-full of water. Investigators thought that it would be an ideal place to get rid of the murder weapon or weapons, as it was just 30 or so yards from the graves.

The investigators brought out a couple of powerful magnets and tied them to a rope. They lowered them into the hole hoping to hook on to the shotgun and pistol. At first, they had some difficulty getting the magnet to the bottom because of various roots that had grown in the shaft, but they finally hit the bottom. They fished around for an hour or so, but no luck.

The investigation did reveal a new piece of the puzzle. The mud found under Spencer's Dodge Dart matched the red clay from the Rifle Club. That meant that Spencer must have driven to the Club and someone else drove his car back to the Eastgate Mall parking lot.

Now, there was an answer to the question, "Where's Rick?" The next question was, "Who did it?"

Laid To Rest

It was a very sad day for the victims' families as both young men were buried on Friday, November 29, 1974. The afternoon was cool and a slight wind was blowing as the first of the two services began. Steve Cannon's graveside service started at 2:30 at the National Cemetery in Chattanooga that had been established during the Civil War due to the heavy losses of Union troops during the various battles fought around the area. It would be the final resting place for this young man. He was buried there because his father had served as a naval officer.

Rick Spencer's funeral service was held at the West Chapel of the Chattanooga Funeral Home. Pastors from his church in Woodmore officiated at the service. His coffin was draped with an American flag. He was honored for his service in the U.S. Army and recognized for his participation at the church in his younger days. At the conclusion of the service, the flag was folded and handed to his mother.

After the service, Rick's casket was carried outside and loaded into a black Cadillac hearse. Friends and family got into their cars and became part of the funeral procession that was led by two Chattanooga motorcycle police officers as they traveled across town to the banks of the Chickamauga Creek.

A few words were spoken at the graveside and Rick Spencer was laid to rest at Lakewood Memory Garden Cemetery, about a mile from where he'd grown up. He was entombed in the mausoleum next to his father, Harry. Taps was played at the conclusion of the graveside service.

The friends and relatives of both men kept wondering who could have done such a thing. They didn't have long to wait.

Logan Comes Clean

John Logan had been a wrestler in high school and he was no stranger to the anxiety of preparing to meet his opponent. Wrestling is a one-on-one sport that requires strength, quickness, agility, and strategy. As the match gets nearer, the butterflies start churning. So Logan was used to the nerves associated with stress, but he'd never experienced anything like what he'd been living with for the past six weeks.

Since that night on October 17, he hadn't been able to sleep without the use of drugs, which sometimes led to horrific nightmares. Seeing the bodies at the Rifle Club on that fateful Wednesday night had just about put him over the edge. Thanksgiving with his family hadn't helped. In fact, it'd only made things worse. He felt sorry for the families of Spencer and Cannon. The guilt and sadness had become too much to deal with. After the family dinner, he told his brother Carl, "I can't take it anymore. I'm going to the cops and tell them everything!"

Friday afternoon, John Logan called TBI Agent Hannah and arranged to meet him at the TBI temporary headquarters at the Holiday Inn in East Ridge. It was a short drive from Logan's apartment. He parked in front of the room that Hannah had given him. Logan knocked on the door and Hannah opened it, inviting him in. Logan took a seat and before Hannah could say anything, Logan said he wanted to turn himself in and began to bare his soul to the agent. When he was finished, he asked to use the bathroom and went in and threw up in the toilet.

Logan had given him the whole story about what happened on that night in October. He signed a statement confirming what he'd said. He alleged that Joe Dyer shot both men with a shotgun. This wouldn't surprise too many people. Logan was then taken down to the city jail and booked as an accomplice in the murder.

With Logan behind bars, the detectives immediately set off on their way to Dyer's house.

Chapter 7—The Arrest

Two detectives had been sitting in a car across the street from 807 Belvoir Crest Drive since midnight. They'd been watching the framed hardboard-siding house that sat on about a third of an acre. A little before six a.m. on Saturday, they were joined by several other officers. The squad encircled the house, while the lead detective and District Attorney Gary Gerbitz knocked on the front door.

A drowsy Mr. Dyer Jr., answered the door. He was shocked by the early-morning visit—especially after he was promptly presented with an arrest warrant for his son and a search warrant for the house and property.

The detective asked, "Is your son here?"

"Yes." He led the detective back to Joe's room.

Joseph P. Dyer III was woken up and told to get dressed. Then he was handcuffed and led out of the house to one of the patrol cars. His mother, still in her night clothes and wearing a bathrobe, cried as she watched her son being escorted out of the house.

The investigators entered the house and began looking for evidence related to the murder. While two detectives searched the young Joe Dyer's room, two officers went to search the basement. It ran the full length of the house. One room covered about half of the basement. The door to the room was locked with a deadbolt. One of the detectives went upstairs and asked Joe's father why the door was locked. He replied, "It's Joe's room."

"Well, do you have a key?"

The senior Dyer went into kitchen and came back with a key.

The police were shocked by what they saw.

In the locked room, they found a small arsenal. The collection included rifles, pistols, and ammunition, along with various weapons that ranged from hunting knives to the barrel of a machine gun. There was even equipment and supplies for loading spent brass casings and shotgun shells. There was no M1 carbine or shotgun, but plenty of shotgun shells. The detectives confiscated a number of items from the basement to be taken to the crime lab for further evaluation.

The search of Joe Dyer's room and the rest of the house didn't turn up anything else. But examining the grounds around the house, one of the officers saw a drainage pipe that looked like it had something stuck in it. On his hands and knees, he peered into the four-inch pipe. Something odd-looking was in there all right, but it was too dark to tell what it was.

He went back to his car, retrieved a flashlight, and returned to the pipe. Sure enough, there was something there and it looked like a smaller pipe. He reached in and pulled out the short barrel of a rifle. He was no firearms expert, but he believed it was an M1 carbine. As he took a closer look at it, he noticed that the serial numbers had been filed off.

There was little doubt in his mind that it was Spencer's M1, which would certainly link Dyer to the murders. Obviously, Dyer had been trying to hide it.

As the search of the property continued, the patrol car with Joe Dyer arrived at the county jail. He was greeted by several law-enforcement officers and Sheriff Frank Newell, one of the leaders of the investigation. The press was also there. As Dyer exited the car in handcuffs, the cameras started flashing. He attempted to cover his head with his coat to conceal his face as he was led into the building by a couple of uniformed police officers.

By noon on Saturday, John Logan and Joe Dyer were booked for the murders of Rick Spencer and Steve Cannon. They were each charged with two counts of murder and two counts of armed robbery. Bond was set at $10,000 each for the robbery charge. No bond was set for the murder charge, meaning the two would be staying in jail until the trial.

The preliminary hearing was scheduled for December 2.

The Grand Jury

It was Monday December 2. Dyer and Logan's preliminary hearing was scheduled for that afternoon. The purpose of this hearing was to determine if there was enough evidence to turn the case over to the grand jury.

Joe Dyer was ready for his first appearance in court. He had a fresh haircut; his black hair was cut short, so it didn't touch his collar in the back, and his sideburns had been trimmed to line up with the bottom of his ears. He was wearing black-rimmed glasses and wore a patterned blue blazer, a big collared shirt, a wide tie, dark trousers, and spit-shined black shoes. Just after one p.m., he stepped out of the Hamilton County jail in handcuffs. He was flanked by a police officer on one side and his father on the other. Each held on to his arm. Several other officers walked behind and in front of him as the entourage made its way slowly toward the Hamilton County Courthouse.

As he walked, Joe looked straight ahead and showed no emotion.

They entered the courthouse and walked down the hallway. Not a word was spoken; only their footsteps echoing off the marble floor made a sound. They walked up the stone stairs and when they reached the courtroom, Joe took a seat next to his lawyer, Joe Wagner. His codefendant, John Logan, was already seated next to his own attorney. He too had a recent haircut and was dressed in his Sunday best.

Wagner had been out of town and hadn't had time to prepare for the hearing, which he asked the court to reschedule. After a brief discussion, the judge granted the request. The hearing was reset for mid-December. Sessions Court Judge B. Tarleton Bowles would preside over the hearing. After the short proceeding, the two defendants were escorted back to the county jail. Once back in their cells, they changed out of their dress clothes and put on their county-issued jumpsuit and sneakers. The jailer took their courtroom clothes and stored them until the next court appearance.

Over the next several days, Attorney Wagner and Joe Dyer had several meetings. This allowed Wagner to get a better understanding of the case that was before him. He knew he'd be facing a challenge.

On the day of the rescheduled preliminary hearing, once again, the accused dressed in their Sunday best and were escorted to the courthouse. It was a full courtroom as the judge called the court to order.

TBI Agent Hannah provided most of the testimony. He recounted the statement given to him by Logan about how Dyer shot and killed both men with a shotgun. He explained the reason for the killing, that Spencer refused to pay for the lost drugs from the drug store break-in. Hannah also described how Dyer had set up a fake drug deal to get Spencer to the Rifle Club. Unfortunately, Steve Cannon was just along for the ride.

At the end of the testimonies, Judge Bowles said, "It appears to the court that the deceased were lured to the scene by the defendants and virtually executed." He then ordered, "for the safety of the community," that the two men be held without bond pending a grand-jury investigation into the case.

On December 18, the grand jury heard the case. It didn't take them long; in less than an hour, they gave their opinion. The accused, Joe Dyer and John Logan, would each be indicted on two counts of murder and two counts of armed robbery. No one in the courtroom was surprised by the decision.

As the hearing ended, the two were handcuffed and the police officers escorted them back to jail, where they would stay until their trial. But law-enforcement officers were still working on the case and had uncovered some new evidence that would have a big impact.

Five days later, a special session of the grand jury was reconvened to review the new information concerning the Rifle Club murders. A third man was brought before this special session in connection with the murders of Spencer and Cannon. It was Donald C. Grimes, Jr. Based on the testimony of the lead investigator, Grimes too was indicted on two counts of murder and two counts of armed robbery. Several hours after the indictment was handed down, around 6:30 p.m., state and county lawmen arrested Donald C. Grimes Jr. at his parent's home. He was booked on the charges at the county jail.

The indictment came as no real surprise to family, friends, and those familiar with the case. As a matter of fact, most wondered why Grimes hadn't been arrested along with Dyer and Logan. After all, the three of them were often seen together with Spencer, as Grimes was considered a member of the Pot and Gun Gang. Some speculated that it might have been because he was away at school. Whatever the reason, he joined his two friends in jail.

The three spent Christmas behind bars, while the Spencer and Cannon families were at home continuing to grieve the loss of Rick and Steve. Lillie Spencer went to church on Christmas Eve, but she couldn't help but think about last years' service when Rick had gone with her after being discharged from the Army. At that time, she was so happy and thankful that he'd returned safely from Vietnam. Now he was gone. She wondered how he could have survived the brutality of war, but not even a year of life back home. As the choir sang "Silent Night," she broke down and cried, then cried the rest of the night.

Christmas at the Cannon house was a solemn day, as Steve's parents remembered that this time last year he was still in high school. Steve had always enjoyed Christmas and they had fond memories of the big smile on his face as he opened his gifts. They would always cherish his smile. However, it would be almost a year before the trial, which meant that Lillie Spencer and the Cannons would have to wait before they could have some kind of closure of the tragedy.

The two families weren't the only ones who were anxious to find out what really happened on that night in October. The city wanted to know more about the Rifle Club murders. Chattanoogans would also have to wait for what some believed would be the trial of the decade.

As they waited, there was another surprising turn of events.

The Wait

The three men charged in the double murder waited out the year to stand trial. But the lines had been drawn during the preliminary and grand-jury hearings. It appeared that the trial would come down to Dyer and Grimes versus Logan. As the three sat in jail, the defendants worked on fine tuning their respective legal representation.

From this point on, Jerry Summers would join Wagner as Dyer's defense team, with Summers taking the lead in representing Dyer. Bill Ortwein would be the primary attorney representing Grimes. Summers and Ortwein knew each other well. Both had gone to Chattanooga Central High School and the University of Tennessee Law School. Also, both had worked for a few years in the District Attorney's office. In their mid-30s, they were considered up-and-coming attorneys in the area. It was a good choice for both defendants. If anyone could structure a sound defense strategy, it would be these two lawyers.

John Logan would continue to be represented by Bob Batson and Dan Poole. Batson had recently worked in the District Attorney's office and Poole had been a partner with the current District Attorney, Gary Gerbitz. It was becoming clear; Logan was teaming up with the prosecution.

The three men were all indicted on the same charges, but John Logan was kept isolated from Dyer and Grimes. After all, it was Logan's statements to authorities that had gotten them thrown in jail and facing the death penalty.

The three young men had to adjust to life behind bars. They passed the time reading, exercising, watching TV, or just daydreaming. Chip Grimes thought about his time at Auburn and how much he missed the things he took for granted, such as going to class. John Logan remembered how good life had been when he was winning wrestling matches and how he should have continued his career in college.

Joe Dyer thought about what would have been if he hadn't gotten kicked out of UT and finished his degree. He'd probably have a real job and wouldn't have had time for the drugs and the other destructive pastimes. He did have a desire to move forward and while waiting on the trial, he took correspondence classes and earned a Bachelor of Arts degree from the University of Tennessee. Even though the school work had kept Joe busy, he and the others wondered what was going on in the outside world.

One piece of news that got the boys' attention was the Vietnam War. By the end of April, the war finally came to an end with the fall of Saigon. The North Vietnamese had taken Saigon, resulting in a mass evacuation of the remaining

American troops, diplomats, and some South Vietnamese civilians desperate to escape from the wrath of the communists. With the country's capital now in the hands of the North, the South Vietnamese government unconditionally surrendered. The communists had prevailed and the Americans had lost this war against communism. The news caused Dyer, Grimes, and Logan to think about Rick Spencer.

As summer approached, they also thought about the parties they were missing. The party circuit continued. Occasionally, there was talk about the murders and the upcoming trial. Some wondered out loud how Dyer got the drop on Spencer, a Vietnam vet and skilled marksman. Others talked about how the mild-mannered Grimes got mixed up in it and how Logan, the athlete, became buddies with a group of non-jock druggies. Most admitted that the Pot and Gun Gang was an odd mix of personalities and backgrounds. The partiers, like most Chattanoogans, anxiously awaited the start of the trial.

Beside the normal party scene, there was plenty going on during the summer. People in Chattanooga and around the country stood in lines to see Universal Pictures' newest release, *Jaws*. The city also had an impressive lineup of rock and roll concerts. These were headlined by the likes of Lynyrd Skynyrd, the Marshall Tucker Band, the Bee Gees, Jethro Tull, and Kiss. Chickamauga Lake was busy as ever, with all types of water sports and plenty of girls in bikinis.

Logan Cuts a Deal

Meanwhile, John Logan's attorneys had been working on a deal with the District Attorney's office. After several months of negotiating, the two sides reached an agreement. Logan had been charged the same as Dyer and Grimes, for the murders and armed robbery. The state agreed to allow Logan to plead guilty to a lesser charge in exchange for his testimony. This meant that he would be taking the witness stand and telling the whole story about the Rifle Club murders.

The first-degree-murder charge was changed to being an accessory to murder. The reduced charge allowed him to post a bond and he was bailed out of jail. By the end of July, the state's key witness in the Spencer and Cannon murder trial was free, pending sentencing on the reduced charge.

John Logan was thankful to be out. Based on the advice of his attorneys, he kept a low profile and stayed out of trouble. He didn't as much as jaywalk across the street. Logan still had the trial in front of him and was anxious to get it over with.

Chapter 8—The Trial Begins

The trial was set to begin on October 15, 1975. Judge Joseph DiRisio was on the bench. The jury of six men and six women, plus two alternates, had been seated and both sides were ready. On the day the trial was scheduled to begin, the defendants, as always dressed in their Sunday best, were brought into the courtroom. As expected, the courtroom was packed with spectators and the news media.

Just after the judge called the court to order, the defense attorneys asked to approach the bench, which the judge granted. As they stood before the judge, they expressed a concern. The words "Judas Logan" had been written on a towel dispenser in the jury's bathroom, which might influence the outcome. The defense attorneys were afraid that it would be prejudicial to their clients and wanted to discuss the matter with the judge.

Judge DiRisio agreed and asked all the attorneys involved in the trial to join him in his chambers. After a relatively brief conversation, they were all in agreement that rescheduling the trial was in the best interest of all parties.

They returned to the courtroom and Judge DiRisio dismissed the jury. The much-anticipated trial was rescheduled for two months hence, on December 9. A new jury would have to be selected. The defendants were returned to jail and the wait continued.

The day after the postponement, one of the custodians for the building told the judge that the slogan "Judas Logan" had been there for several weeks, if not longer. He'd already removed it, so it wouldn't happen again.

The trial resumed on December 9. The new jury consisted of eight men and four women. They were racially balanced— six black and six white jurors. The trial itself began the morning of the next day with opening statements from both sides. The city was holding its collective breath.

Opening Statements

The historical Hamilton County Courthouse is on the corner of Georgia Avenue and East 7th Street, right in the center of the downtown Chattanooga. The three-story structure is built out of Tennessee limestone and concrete. It was completed in 1913. The south front has a large porch with four tall Corinthian columns rising from the porch to a header at the roof line. Inside, the center of the building features a magnificent three-story rotunda with a stained-glass dome. The walkways and stairs are covered with white marble. The so-called Rifle Club Murder trial was taking place in the grand old building.

On Wednesday, December 10, 1975, Joe Dyer and Chip Grimes were escorted from the jail to the courthouse. Dyer was once again dressed in the patterned blue blazer and a wide tie. Grimes was wearing glasses, which looked like clear aviation glasses, and a checked sports coat, along with a wide tie. Both men had recent haircuts. Joe Dyer's mother accompanied him and a handful of law-enforcement officers. The entourage walked into the courthouse, up the stairs, down the hall, and into the courtroom. The defendants sat down next to their attorneys.

The criminal-court judge entered the packed courtroom. The bailiff stated in a deep baritone voice, "All rise. This court is now in session. The honorable Judge Joseph DiRisio is presiding."

The judge sat, then said, "You may be seated."

82

WHERE'S RICK?

Every seat in the gallery was taken and people were standing wherever they could. The hallways of the grand old building were also jammed with onlookers, as well as TV, radio, and newspaper reporters accompanied by their support crews. Media trucks and cars were parked outside along the curbs that ran beside the sidewalks encircling the large white structure.

Many believed it was the biggest trial Chattanooga had seen since 1964, when Jimmy Hoffa was on trial in federal court for jury tampering. Hoffa was convicted of two of three counts of trying to bribe a 1962 federal-court jury in Nashville. He was sentenced to eight years in prison, but served less than five. Ironically, Jimmy Hoffa had gone missing earlier this year and hadn't been seen since July 1975. While the Rifle Club Murders didn't garner the national attention that the Hoffa trial did, there was certainly more interest locally.

Judge DiRisio outlined the conditions of the trial, along with his expectations. He made it clear that there would be no outbursts from the gallery and expected an orderly courtroom.

Then the bailiff read the charges.

Joseph P. Dyer III and Donald C. Grimes, Jr., were charged in the deaths of Rick Spencer and Steve Cannon at the Chattanooga Rifle Club. The two were also charged with armed robbery of the deceased men.

Stan Lanzo and Dave Rotroff, Assistant District Attorneys, sat at the prosecution's table and would manage most of the work for the state. Their boss Gary Gerbitz, the District Attorney, sat behind them in the front row of the gallery. Jerry Summers was representing Joe Dyer and Bill Ortwein served as legal counsel for Grimes.

The judge told the prosecutors, "You may address the jury."

Stan Lanzo stood up and walked to the jury box. His statement was short and to the point. He said, "Ladies and gentlemen of the jury, we will show you, without a doubt, that these two men are guilty of ambushing and shooting down

Rick Spencer and Steve Cannon in a hail of bullets, then stealing their money. John Logan will tell you exactly what occurred on that horrific night. We thank you for your service." He then returned to his seat.

Next it was Jerry Summers's turn and it didn't take long for the fireworks to explode. During Summers's opening statement, he said, "John Logan is without question a liar. He has made a deal with the District Attorney's office and my client is innocent." He went on to say, "The credibility of Logan is the real heart of the case." Summers returned to the defense's table and it was Bill Ortwein's turn.

He, too, attacked Logan's credibility. It became obvious that he and Summers had become allies in the defense of their clients. Summers would take the lead in the defense's case.

Both sides had staked out their strategies. The prosecutors were using Logan as their primary witness. The defense's job was to attack Logan every chance they could. They got their first chance the very next day, as Logan was scheduled to take the stand.

How It Happened

The prosecutors got things going by calling several of Spencer's friends to the stand to discuss aspects of Spencer and his relationship with the defendants. Dave Prickett, one of Spencer's roommates, took the stand. He talked about Rick's involvement with drugs as a dealer. He said that Spencer had been selling marijuana and pills since the beginning of the summer of 1974. By August, Rick's drug business was booming and he was making a lot of money.

When asked about Spencer's relationship with Dyer, Logan, and Grimes, Prickett said, "They were good friends. They spent a lot of time together. They hung out a lot at our apartment, they partied together, and they frequently went to the Rifle Club for target practice. The four also smoked a lot of pot together and Dyer, Logan, and Grimes even became surrogate salesmen for Rick's drug business."

"As far as you know, did Joe Dyer carry a gun when he wasn't at the Club?"

Prickett replied, "Yes. When he came over to our place, he always had a pistol with him and when asked about it, he'd say it was for protection. Then he'd add that he wasn't afraid to use it."

The Assistant DA had a few more questions. "Did you ever hear Dyer talk about the Drew's Drugs Store break in?"

Again, Prickett replied in the affirmative. "Yes. A day or two after it happened, he came to our place bragging about how big a score it was."

Lanzo asked, "When did you last see Rick Spencer?"

"October 17, 1974."

"Did you go looking for him?"

"Jim Lewis and I asked around to see if anyone had seen him and had no luck. We both felt that Joe Dyer had something to do with it, because Rick was supposed to meet him at the Rifle Club on the night he went missing for the fake drug deal. So on Sunday, we went to see Logan and Dyer to ask them if they knew anything about Rick's disappearance. They both said that they hadn't seen him, but we didn't believe them."

Lanzo had a follow-up question. "Do you still think Dyer had something to do with Spencer and Cannon's disappearance?"

Prickett, said, "Yes sir!"

"No more questions."

The defense attorneys had few questions for Prickett.

With the questioning over, Prickett returned to his seat and Carl Logan was called to the stand. He gave an overview of his brother's involvement with the Pot and Gun Gang. The younger Logan also explained that Grimes and Dyer were often at his apartment and many times they crashed there.

He talked about the afternoon of October 17 when Chip Grimes ran checks through the check-writing machine. Carl also testified that Joe Dyer asked for his .45 pistol and changed out the ammunition, which he thought was odd at the time. But he was glad he did, because that move linked Dyer to the murders.

When asked what he did that night after the gang left, he said, "I stayed at the apartment. Some friends came over and we watched TV."

The prosecutor finished up his questioning and the defense asked a few more, then Carl Logan went back to his seat.

The county coroner and medical examiner, Dr. George Beckmann, was called next to testify. He was asked to describe the condition of the bodies when he examined them.

The doctor said, "When they got to the morgue, they were badly decomposed. That, combined with their wounds, made the corpses completely unidentifiable, so we had to get their dentists in to identify them based on their dental records. The dentists confirmed that the bodies were those of Rick Spencer and Steve Cannon."

The coroner continued to describe the nature of their injuries. "Portions of the heads of both Spencer and Cannon had been blown away. The back of Spencer's head was missing and the right side of Cannon's face was gone. Both wounds were caused by a short-range shotgun blast."

Lanzo then asked, "Just how close is short range?"

Beckmann replied, "Two or three feet." He then went on to describe the other wounds. He talked about the three shotgun wounds to Spencer's upper body. Next, he talked about

86

Cannon's wounds, that he had a two-inch hole in his chest, which had also come from a close-range shot. The young man also had a bullet wound in his back between the shoulder blades. Beckmann said, "Most likely, the bullet to the back knocked Cannon down and the shotgun was used to execute him."

Beckmann also testified that he'd removed the shotgun pellets from both bodies and the bullet from Cannon. He'd turned them over to the county crime lab. Their ballistic technicians had determined the murder weapons were a model 97 Winchester shotgun and a .45 automatic pistol. He went on to say that the killing of the two men was one of the most horrific that he'd ever witnessed during his time as the county coroner. Beckmann's testimony was a sobering recollection of the brutality of the murders.

A chemist with the Atlanta branch of the Bureau of Alcohol, Tobacco, and Firearms was called to the stand. He testified that the 45-caliber slug taken from Cannon's body matched the chemical makeup of bullets taken from Dyer's basement.

While the chemist was a matter-of-fact witness, the next witness struck the emotions of everyone in the courtroom.

Steve Cannon's Dad Addresses the Jury

Jim Cannon, Steve's father and a retired naval officer, was called to the witness stand. He described the fateful day. It was midafternoon on October 17, 1974, when he dropped Steve off at Rick's apartment. Little did he know at the time that would be the last time he would see his son alive. He also described how he and his wife waited that night for Steve and Rick to join them for dinner, but they never showed up.

"Steve didn't come home that night and when I didn't hear from him by mid-morning, I became worried and called Rick's apartment. One of his roommates said that Rick wasn't there and hadn't been seen since yesterday afternoon. The last time they saw Steve was when he left with Rick."

Jim Cannon then described how, over the next couple of days, he made dozens of phones calls to Steve's friends. He also drove all over Hamilton County and north Georgia looking for his son. He continued to carry on his own search, while helping the police as they looked for the missing pair. He kept his hopes up until the bodies were found in late November 1974. By the time he finished telling his story, there weren't many dry eyes in the gallery or the jury box. But the roiling emotions were just getting started.

Logan Takes the Stand

The bailiff asked Logan to raise his right hand and place his other hand on the Bible and repeat, "I, John Gerald Logan, swear that the testimony I'm about to give is the truth, the whole truth, and nothing but the truth, so help me God." The court officer tucked the Bible under his arm and returned to his seat. Logan sat down.

Then, the state's key witness was asked by the prosecutor to tell the jury what happened on the night of October 17, 1974.

Logan cleared his throat and started recounting that day. "Chip Grimes had come into town the night before, because he needed some money. He'd gotten into some trouble while attending Auburn University and needed to pay for a lawyer in Alabama. The fastest way for him to get the money he needed was to cash some of the cashier's checks we'd stolen from the drugstore."

"So Thursday morning, the three of us, Joe Dyer, Chip Grimes, and I, met at my apartment. We'd hidden the checks in the woods at the Rifle Club and drove out there to retrieve them. We then drove downtown to Meyer Business Machines and bought a Paymaster check-writing machine. On the way back to my apartment, we stopped at Leonard's and got a cheeseburger and beer. During lunch, Chip gave us the details about his problems in Alabama. After lunch we went to my apartment."

At this point, Grimes' attorney interrupted the testimony and asked to speak to the judge. He approached the bench, along with Summers and the prosecutor. He told the judge that he wanted to file a motion for a mistrial.

Judge DiRisio asked, "On what basis?"

Ortwein said, "Logan introduced a pending legal matter in Auburn, Alabama, and that comment might influence the jury."

At that point, the judge called for a recess and said, "We'll adjourn for lunch and reconvene at one o'clock." He asked the attorneys to join him in his chambers. After a brief discussion, DiRisio denied the motion.

During the break, the jury returned to the jury room and were served lunch. The defendants went to the courthouse's holding cell and ate a sandwich. Most of the other spectators left the courtroom and went to get something to eat. A few went to the Krystal on the corner of Cherry Street. Others walked across the street to the Brass Register. It was a favorite eatery and bar. The conversation in the Register was loud, as most of the tables were discussing the testimonies from the morning session. Almost everyone had already formulated an opinion as to who was guilty.

Just after one, the jury filed back into the courtroom and the court was called to order. Logan stepped back in the witness box, took his seat, and continued his account of October 17.

"When we arrived at my apartment, my brother Carl was there watching TV in the back room. Grimes went into the kitchen and began running checks through the writer. I went to my bedroom and took a nap, while Joe stayed in the living room doing something.

"When I got up, I joined Dyer in the living room and a few minutes later, Chip finished with the checks, and we went into the kitchen. Joe began talking about the money Spencer owed us from the lost pills.

"Dyer was insistent about getting the money back from Spencer. It didn't bother me and Chip that much, but it was a real sore spot for Joe, and he had a plan to get the money from Spencer. He began to explain his plan.

"Joe had met with Spencer a week earlier to tell him about a drug deal with a guy by the name of John Fry. Fry had been selling pot in Chattanooga for a couple of years. He'd gone to Notre Dame High School and I knew him, but I hadn't seen him but a couple of times since graduation.

"Dyer told Spencer that Fry was going to sell him ten pounds of marijuana for a thousand dollars. Rick was good with the deal and told Dyer just to let him know when and where he'd meet Fry. Dyer told Spencer he'd let him know and would go along to make the introduction. Rick was okay with Dyer being there.

"The truth was that John Fry had not been contacted about any kind of a pot deal involving Spencer or Dyer. As a matter a fact, Joe Dyer didn't even know John Fry, but used his name, because he thought that Spencer would recognize him as a drug dealer, which would make him think that it was a legitimate deal. The whole story was concocted by Dyer to get Spencer to the Rifle Club with a pocketful of money."

Logan continued, "Dyer kept explaining the plan and said, 'We'll go to Spencer's and tell him the Fry deal is on. Then the three of us and Spencer will meet at the Rifle Club. Once we're all there, we'll act like we're waiting on Fry. Then Dyer would force Spencer to give him the money he owed.

"I didn't like the idea and didn't want to go, but Dyer insisted. Reluctantly, I went along. As we got into the car, we were armed. Grimes had my brother's forty-five, Dyer had a shotgun, and I had a nine-millimeter pistol. As we left my apartment, Dyer said, 'Let's go get our money back!'

"We stopped by Spencer's place. We pulled into the driveway. Spencer walked out to greet us. We didn't get out of the car. Dyer told him the deal was on and Spencer said he'd meet us at the Rifle Club. He said he'd be right behind us.

"It was only a twelve-mile drive to the Rifle Club. On the way, not much was said between the three of us. I just kept visualizing how this was going to work. I wondered what the outcome would be, because both Dyer and Spencer were strong-willed guys. I knew something had to give, which most likely wouldn't be good.

"It was dark when we turned off Hunter Road on to the gravel drive and up the small hill to the gate of the Rifle Club. The gate was locked and Dyer handed me the key. I got out and under the light from the headlights unlocked the gate. Joe told me to leave the gate open, because Spencer was on his way. I got back in the car and we drove into the Club.

"We drove on the driveway that ran beside the meadow on the left and parked on the gravel parking lot. We got out of the car armed with our guns. It wasn't unusual for us to have guns on a drug deal, just as added protection. We walked to the left of the parking lot into woods, then into a small clearing. In the middle of the clearing was a rock-lined campfire pit. It was a regular meeting place when we came to the Rifle Club.

91

"Once in the clearing, Dyer again outlined the plan, this time with more detail. He said when Spencer got there, I would fire up a pipe of marijuana and offer it to him. We'd pass the pipe around and after a couple of tokes, Joe would point the shotgun at Spencer and demand the money. He didn't mention what would happen if Rick didn't hand the money over.

"We'd been there about ten minutes when we saw headlights bobbing up and down as a car rolled slowly along the gravel drive into the parking area. The car stopped, the lights went off, and two guys got out and headed to the clearing. We could see the silhouette of Spencer leading the way. He was carrying his M1 carbine and Steve Cannon followed closely behind. We were surprised to see Steve.

"Once in the clearing, Spencer asked, 'Where's the drug guy?'

"Dyer replied, 'He's not here yet, but he's on the way. Why don't we smoke a bowl? I'm sure he'll be here soon.'

"Taking the cue, I fired up a pipe. Spencer turned to Cannon, handed him his M1, and told him to go the edge of meadow and keep a lookout. The youngster took the rifle and walked off through the woods.

"We sat on the ground and passed around the pipe. Ten minutes went by and still no pot dealer. The four of us kept smoking and Spencer started telling stories about his time in Vietnam. Dyer was always fascinated with them. After about thirty minutes, Spencer stopped talking and stood up. He looked at Dyer and said, 'This guy isn't coming and we're leaving.' He then gave a loud whistle and a few minutes later Cannon appeared from the woods and stepped into the clearing. He walked up to Spencer and handed him the M1, and Rick told him that they were leaving, because the pot guy didn't show up.

"I started walking toward the parking lot. Cannon was next in line about twenty feet behind me, followed by Spencer. Dyer and Grimes brought up the rear. As they walked Dyer was apologizing to Spencer for the guy not showing up. I was thinking, 'Man, I'm glad it didn't come to a confrontation.' I guessed Dyer changed his mind. It must have been the Vietnam stories.'

"Then all of a sudden, all hell broke loose.

"The first shot sounded like a bomb going off, which was followed by a continuous series of explosions lasting three or four seconds. I was shocked and I turned around just in time to see Cannon hit the ground and Spencer falling. Cannon was lying face up and Grimes was clutching his pistol with both hands as smoke eased from the barrel of his gun. Steve had been shot in the back as he began to run toward the parking lot.

"Dyer's first shot hit Spencer in the left arm, which in effect disarmed him. He'd been carrying the carbine in his left hand. The shotgun blast caused Rick to drop his gun and it sent him spinning to the ground. Dyer then shot him in the right arm. Spencer was lying face down on the ground and was muttering something as Dyer rushed up to him. He aimed his shotgun at the back of his head and pulled the trigger. The back of the man's head was gone in an instant.

"With Spencer dead, Dyer wanted to make sure Cannon was done as well. The young man was lying on the ground face up. He was softly moaning and his eyes were closed. Dyer walked over to him and at point blank range fired the buckshot into his chest, but he wasn't done and shot him again, this time on the right side of his face. The blast made him almost unrecognizable.

"The gunfire filled the air with smoke, which was accompanied by the sulfuric smell of gunpower. Not a word was spoken for a few moments until I asked Dyer, 'Why did you have to do that?'

93

"Dyer replied, 'I had to, or Spencer would get me back for taking the money.'

"Grimes wanted to leave the scene right then and said, 'Let's get the hell out of here!' I wanted to leave as well, but Dyer said, 'No, we have to do something with these bodies.'

"From that point on, Dyer calmly took control and orchestrated the cleanup. He ordered me to drag Spencer's body into the woods and find a place where we could bury him. He then asked Grimes to walk over to the Club's maintenance shed and see if he could find a shovel or something, so we could dig a hole. Thanks to Dyer's planning, each of us had a flashlight, which came in handy as we walked through the woods.

"I dragged Spencer's body into the woods for about thirty feet and stopped. I left the body on the ground and went further into the darkness to scout out a place where we could dig a hole. Another fifty feet into the woods, I found a place that looked suitable for a grave. It was a small opening in the woods and didn't look like there were too many tree roots around. I yelled at Dyer that I'd found a place and he started heading that way, dragging Cannon's body. He then yelled at me to get the money out of Spencer's pockets.

"I moved Spencer near the burial spot I'd picked out and began going through his pockets, looking for the money. It was all I could do to keep from throwing up at the sight of the bloody body. It was horrific. I went through all his pockets and pulled out the money. It was mostly twenties, but there were some hundreds and a few fifties as well. I didn't count it, but it was a lot of money, I'm guessing well over a thousand. I stuffed the money in my pockets.

"I could hear Dyer and Grimes coming through the woods, then I stared down at Spencer's body and was thankful that it wasn't me lying on the ground. The other two arrived. Grimes had found a shovel and a pick at the maintenance shed. Chip handed me the pick and we started digging. But as we started, Dyer said, 'Just dig one hole. We don't have time to dig two graves. We'll just throw them both in, one on top of the other. The fewer graves we dig, the less likely someone will find them.'

"It was slow digging in the red clay, but we kept digging as fast as we could, because we wanted to get out of there as soon as possible. While we dug, Dyer began to strip the corpses of their clothes. When he was finished, the two were left lying on the ground in nothing but their underpants and socks. After he'd undressed them, he knelt beside them for a few minutes, just staring at them. I thought it was a bit odd, but I didn't say anything.

"During the undressing, Dyer had retrieved each man's billfold and Spencer's car keys. He'd put them in his pocket. He took the clothes and tossed them randomly into the woods as he walked back to the clearing. He assumed the leaves would cover them before anyone noticed them.

"We continued the digging until the hole was about two feet wide, about two feet deep, and about six feet long. The two bodies were put in the hole. Cannon went in first, then we threw Spencer on top. It was somewhat of a tight fit, but it would have to do. We threw dirt on top of them and spread the excess around on the ground, so there wouldn't be a noticeable mound. Then we covered the grave with leaves. By the dark of night, it looked like we'd covered up the grave fairly well. We carried the digging tools with us as we jogged back to the clearing.

"When we got back to the clearing, Dyer was sitting on the ground looking through the wallets he'd collected from the dead men. Spencer's M1 carbine was next to him. I asked him why he took their clothes off. Dyer's response was that he believed if the bodies were found in two or three years, they'd

95

be hard to identify without clothes. My next question was, 'What are your going to do with the carbine?'

Dyer replied, 'I'll take it home, file off the serial number, so it can't be traced, and add it to my collection.'

"I then handed Dyer all the money I'd recovered from Spencer. Dyer counted it and handed me a hundred and thirty dollars. He said that was my share. I didn't say anything. I just took the money and stuffed it into the front pocket of my jeans.

"Then Dyer, still in command, laid out the next steps. Grimes was to return the tools to the shed. He wanted me to drive Spencer's car to Eastgate Shopping Mall. He told me to park it in the parking lot near the golf course, roll the windows down, and leave the keys in the ignition. I asked him why. Dyer's reason was he hoped the car would be stolen.

"Grimes and Dyer would ride together and pick me up in the mall's parking lot. Dyer tossed me the keys and said, 'Drive the speed limit. You don't want to get pulled over!' I just looked at him and didn't say a word. We were all ready to get out of there.

"I was the first to leave and a few minutes later, Dyer pulled just outside the gate and stopped the car, then Grimes got out and locked the gate. He got back in the car, and they headed to Eastgate. It was about a twenty-minute drive. They drove around the shopping center. I was where I was supposed to be and left the car as I'd been instructed to do. Dyer pulled up next to the red Dodge Dart and I got in the back seat. He said, 'We have a couple more things to do that will put us in the clear.'

"He pulled out of the parking lot onto Brainerd Road heading north. He took a left on South Moore Road and then pulled onto I-24 and headed toward Missionary Ridge. He handed Grimes and me the dead men's billfolds. He told us to toss them out the window. Grimes threw his first, then I flung the other one out into the night. Dyer's logic was if they were found, it would really throw off investigators as to where the dead men were.

"The next stop was my apartment.

"On the way, Dyer said, 'Let's just keep this to ourselves. There's nothing that points to us. Don't tell anybody about it. The story is Spencer never showed up.' He stopped in front of my apartment and I got out. Dyer told Grimes to give me the forty-five and said, 'Give it back to Carl and tell him to clean it up before he stores it away. We don't want anything that can trace it back to us!'

"Dyer said he had one more thing to do after he dropped Chip off. He called Rick's apartment around ten-thirty and asked for Rick. He knew what the answer would be. 'Spencer isn't here.'"

As Logan finished the story, the prosecutor had a few more questions. Lanzo asked him to tell the court about the Drew's Drug break-in, which Logan did.

Next, he asked him about his relationship with Grimes and Dyer. He had become friends with them from parties. He said he and Dyer had become real good friends until the night he tried to make a move on him. Logan went on to explain that Dyer had made a homosexual advance on him one night while they were sharing a bed, but nothing happened. From that point on, they still hung out together, but Logan kept his distance from Dyer.

Lanzo had one last question for Logan. "Is the man who planned the trap for Spencer in the courtroom?"

John Logan said, "Yes," and pointed to Joe Dyer.

As Logan finished his testimony, the silent courtroom started buzzing, mostly from the gallery.

The defense would get their time for cross-examination. But first, another mistrial motion was filed.

Motion for Mistrial

It was Friday morning, October 12, and the second time in two days that the defense filed for a mistrial. Jerry Summers filed the motion late Thursday night after Logan's testimony. It was based on his statement that Dyer had once made a homosexual advance toward him. The judge sent the jury to the jury room following the motion and gave the attorneys time to prepare their arguments on the mistrial motion.

The morning began and the jury stayed in the jury room as both sides gave their comments to the judge concerning yesterday's motion. Jerry Summers called the statement "prejudicial and reversible; this case is being tried under state law, not Freudian concepts."

On the other side, Assistant DA Lanzo argued that such evidence should be allowed. "It's possible that Dyer had something else driving him to commit the alleged murders." Lanzo added, "Let's not forget that Dyer stripped the clothes off the victims and knelt near them for several minutes." The prosecutor finished his remarks by saying, "The statement would not constitute reversible error anyway, since the state's case against Dyer is overwhelming and is going to become even more overwhelming."

Judge DiRisio admitted that the question of whether the evidence should be allowed was "a close one." He went on to say that criminal courts are "hampered by evidentiary rules, despite the fact that what a person does is a function of his whole personality."

The debate between the two sides went back and forth. In the end, the judge denied the motion. His reasoning was based on the fact that the statement by Logan was not elicited intentionally by the state. The criminal-court judge also noted that community standards constantly changed over time and such matters as homosexuality were taken in a more matter-of-fact way than they would have been 50 years ago. The jury was called back and the trial resumed at 12:30 p.m.

Logan returned to the witness stand and the cross-examination by the defense began. The questioning continued through the afternoon. The courtroom had heard what Logan had to say and next they would get to hear Joseph Dyer's side of the story. It would surprise everyone in the courtroom.

Dyer Takes the Stand

It was Saturday, the fifth day of the trial. The courthouse was once again overflowing with spectators and the media as Joseph P. Dyer III took the stand. The bailiff swore him in just as he had with every other witness. After he took his seat, his attorney, Jerry Summers, approached the stand and asked him, "Did you kill Rick Spencer and Steve Cannon?"

Without blinking an eye, the stoic Dyer replied, "No!"

Summers next asked, "Did you rob the bodies?"

"No!"

"Tell the jury what happened on the night of October 17."

Dyer looked at the jury box, took a drink of water, then began his version of the story.

"John Logan and I did arrange to meet Spencer at the Rifle Club for the purchase of marijuana. Chip Grimes was in town for the weekend to attend an engagement party for John Logan and his fiancée. He just went along for the ride and didn't have anything to do with planning the drug deal.

"We were to meet Spencer in the clearing at the Rifle Club around five-thirty in the evening. Logan, Grimes, and I got there first and Spencer and Steve Cannon showed up about ten or fifteen minutes later. Once the five of us were there, we sat down on the ground and started talking, while we waited for the dealer to show up.

"About twenty minutes later, we saw a car driving up the gravel driveway. We thought it was the guy with the pot. It stopped in the parking lot next to Spencer's car. The guy got out and starting walking toward the clearing where we sat. As he got closer, we could see that it wasn't the dealer. It was Carl Logan. He was carrying a shotgun, which he handed to his brother once in the clearing. Carl had a .45 automatic pistol stuck in the front of his pants, with just the handle showing.

"Carl joined the conversation, but soon thereafter, Spencer said, 'I don't think this guy is going to show.' He stood up and started to leave. Cannon followed Spencer's move and they started walking toward the parking lot. John Logan then stood up and said to Spencer, 'I need the money you owe us!'"

Dyer claimed that Logan needed the money to pay for an engagement ring and to pay off his fiancée's medical bills. Spencer refused to pay the money and John got mad and demanded the money.

Dyer continued, "At that point, Logan shot Spencer in the left arm. John then quickly fired several more shots at him. Then Cannon started walking toward Spencer and Carl Logan yelled out a warning. The older Logan shot Cannon in the head. John then emptied the gun into the two men. Then for good measure, Carl Logan fired his forty-five at Cannon as he lay on the ground.

"As the smoke cleared, I was in a state of shock and sat down on the ground and threw up. The two Logans then insisted that we were never to say anything to anyone about what happened."

He said John Logan then took Spencer's body and Carl grabbed Cannon's body and they dragged them to the burial site. Dyer said he and Grimes didn't assist in the burial of the bodies and left the Rifle Club.

Dyer reiterated that John and Carl Logan committed the murders on October 17 and that neither he nor Chip Grimes fired a shot. He continued to point the finger at the Logans by saying they were drug addicts. The defendant added that on the day of the murders, John Logan had been smoking marijuana practically all day.

According to Dyer, Carl Logan used various drugs and tried about everything. Dyer also claimed that one day, he stood in the bathroom door of the Logan's apartment watching both men shoot drugs into their veins. Joseph Dyer continued to paint the picture that the Logans were drug-crazed and most likely out of their minds on the day of the murders.

When asked about the Drew's Drug break-in, Dyer testified that he didn't participate. He also said that he didn't hassle Spencer over the lost pills. He closed his testimony by saying that he and Rick Spencer were good friends and he had no reason to kill him.

As Joe Dyer completed his statement, it was now the Assistant DA's turn for cross-examination. His first comment was, "Mr. Dyer, that was quite a story. I think the only thing that you got right was that John Logan does have a fiancée."

Next Lanzo asked Dyer, "Do you deny being a homosexual?"

Dyer quickly replied, "I certainly do deny it."

"Did you carry a forty-five pistol?"

"Yes, I frequently carry a gun for self-protection."

"Did you set up the drug deal that got Spencer to the Rifle Club on October seventeenth?"

"Yes."

"Now tell me why you went to the Rifle Club."

Joe Dyer looked him in the eye and said, "For Rick's protection."

"Who did you set the drug deal up with?"

"John Fry."

Lanzo continued the cross-examination for an hour or so. As he began to wrap up the questioning, he said, "I want to make sure I've got this right. You were going to the drug deal to protect Rick Spencer. Is that right?"

"Yes."

"What did you do to protect him?"

Dyer hesitated before solemnly replying, "Nothing."

"*You* were what he needed protection from. Isn't that true, Mr. Dyer?" After a pause, Lanzo said, "No more questions."

The Saturday session was over. There were no proceedings scheduled for Sunday and the trial would resume on Monday morning. The judge, lawyers, and jury were looking forward to a day of rest.

The Pot Dealer

On Monday morning, once again, Dyer and Grimes were dressed as if they were going to church. They were escorted from the jail to the courthouse by several police officers. The courthouse was as crowded as it'd been the previous week. Rumors were buzzing around that a surprise witness was going to take the stand. A low roar was heard throughout the courtroom as the anxious gallery chatted about who they expected as the witness.

When Judge DiRisio entered from his chambers, the room became silent, then the bailiff announced, "Please rise. The court is now in session."

The judge asked the courtroom to be seated and asked the prosecutor to call his next witness.

"The state calls John Fry to the stand."

The back doors of the courtroom opened and in walked a young man dressed in a prison jumpsuit. He was escorted by a

Kentucky State Trooper, who led him to the witness box, then took a seat in the gallery. Fry, age 22, was sworn in by the bailiff. Fry had been brought to Chattanooga from the Federal Youth Center in Ashland, Kentucky, where he'd been serving time since January for passing counterfeit money. He was originally from Chattanooga, where his father was an insurance agent, and he'd attended Notre Dame High School.

The Assistant DA began the questioning, "Have you ever sold drugs in Chattanooga?"

Fry answered, "Yes."

"Have you ever sold marijuana in Chattanooga?"

"Yes."

The prosecutor then asked Fry if he knew Joe Dyer.

"I don't know him and to the best of my knowledge, I've never seen him."

Then Lanzo walked over to the defense table and pointed to Joe Dyer. "Have you ever seen this man before?"

"No sir."

"Have you ever talked to him about a drug deal that was to take place at the Chattanooga Rifle Club?"

"No."

"Do you know John and Carl Logan?"

Fry said, "Yes, I knew them from high school, but we didn't hang out together. I've been to their apartment once or twice."

"Did you ever talk to them about a drug deal that was to take place at the Rifle Club?"

"No."

"Did you participate in a marijuana sale on October 17, 1974, at the Chattanooga Rifle Club?"

"No!"

"Have you ever been to the Chattanooga Rifle Club?"

"No. I have no idea where it is."

Lanzo then said, "So that we're clear, you don't know Joseph Dyer and you don't know anything about a drug deal that was to take place at the Chattanooga Rifle Club. Is that correct?"

Fry answered, "Yes, that is correct."

"No more questions, Your Honor." The Assistant DA took his seat.

Judge DiRisio asked Jerry Summers if he had any questions. The defense attorney said, "Yes, Your Honor." He approached the witness stand with a handful of papers. Before he started the questioning, he shuffled through the papers, then paused as he seemed to have found the page he was looking for. He placed it at the top of the stack and began acting as if he was reading it. He then looked at Fry and said, "Mr. Fry, are you a heroin addict?"

Light gasps came from the gallery. Fry seemed stunned by the question, but replied, "Not now."

"Isn't it true that you had a hundred-dollar-a-day heroin habit?"

The witness replied, "Yes, I was addicted to heroin, but I went to Moccasin Bend Psychiatric Hospital and kicked the habit through their drug-treatment program."

"How long have you been involved with drugs, either using them or selling them?"

"I started when I was in high school."

The defense attorney then folded up his papers and said, "No more questions."

The judge dismissed John Fry and the state trooper escorted him out of the courtroom. It had been a short visit in Chattanooga and he was on his way back to Kentucky.

The defense called the next witness, an employee from Moccasin Bend Hospital. A balding middle-aged man took the stand. He was wearing black-rimmed glasses, a blue blazer, a dark-blue shirt, and a bright yellow-pastel tie. Summers asked him where he worked and he said that he worked at the

Moccasin Bend Psychiatric Hospital. The questioning continued, "What do you do there? What's your job?"

"I'm a psychiatrist and I work with people who have drug dependencies."

"Do you know John Fry?"

"Yes."

"Was he a patient there?"

"Yes."

"Would you describe his mental condition based on his medical records?"

He said, "Mr. Fry has an antisocial personality and other mental and emotional problems."

The defense attorney had one more question. "Can you believe what John Fry tells you?"

"Sometimes."

Summers walked back to his table and said, "Thank you. We have no further questions."

Stan Lanzo rose, walked over to the witness box, and asked the psychiatrist, "In your opinion, is Mr. Fry clean today and is he able to know if he knows someone?"

The doctor replied "yes" to both questions. The prosecution had no more questions. The judge dismissed the witness.

Then, in a surprise move, Carl Logan was recalled to the witness stand by the defense. As he took the stand, the judge reminded him that he was still under oath.

Jerry Summers asked him if he had a shotgun.

"Yes."

"When did you purchase it?"

"I bought it in Birmingham, Alabama, on October 29, 1974."

"Do you have a receipt?"

"No."

"Did you own a shotgun before then?"

"No, sir."

The Assistant DA then asked him a series of questions. "Have you ever used heroin or cocaine?"

"No."

"Have you ever taken drugs by injection?"

"No."

"On the afternoon of October 17, did you give your forty-five pistol to Joe Dyer?"

"Yes."

"What did he do with the gun when you gave it to him?"

"He took my bullets out of the pistol and gave them back to me, then he replaced them with his ammunition and handed the gun to Chip Grimes."

"One last question," the prosecutor said. "Where were you on the night of October 17, 1974?"

The younger Logan stated, "I was at my apartment with some friends watching TV."

"No more questions!"

No more witnesses were called to the stand as both sides rested their case. The judge granted a recess and when the trial resumed, each side would give their closing arguments.

Closing Statements

The state was the first to address the jury. It was their job to prove that the defendants were guilty of the charges.

Assistant District Attorneys Dave Rotroff and Stan Lanzo took turns presenting their case to the men and women of the jury. Rotroff stood, walked to the jury box, and started by calling the jury's attention to the corroboration of John Logan's testimony. He pointed out, "Without it, we wouldn't know the background of the story or the details about what really happened at the Rifle Club."

He reviewed the history of what led up to the night of the murders.

"Spencer, Dyer, Grimes, and Logan were friends. Spencer and Dyer had known each other before Rick went off to war. It wasn't until he returned from Vietnam that the four of them developed a strong friendship, a bond that evolved around drugs.

"The four also had an interest in guns and it was not unusual for the four to go to the Chattanooga Rifle Club, where Spencer and Dyer were members, for some target practice. Spencer was the most accomplished of the group on the firing range and was considered an expert marksman by the U.S. Army, but Joe Dyer also had a reputation for being able to handle guns.

"The drug activity started with recreational use and evolved into the drug-dealing business. Spencer took the most active role in the drug distribution. He was the entrepreneur and had the money. The other three were just minor participants in the dealing.

"One night over a couple of joints, Chip Grimes confessed to the gang that he'd gotten into some trouble and needed some money to hire a lawyer. The four were talking about various ways to get some quick money. After some discussion, Drew's Drugs in Dalewood seemed to be an easy target. Spencer had the most knowledge about the store, since he had worked there, but refused to have anything to do with the break-in. The other three liked the idea and developed a plan. They scheduled the robbery around Labor Day of 1974.

"The break-in was a success, as the three got away with cashier's checks and a sack full of pills. A day or two after the burglary, Dyer was heard bragging about it to some friends.

"The three didn't know what to do with the pills, so they asked Spencer to sell them for them, since he had connections in the drug world. Spencer agreed to sell them, but lost some of the pills and refused to pay for the lost drugs. This angered Joe Dyer and he felt that he'd been ripped off.

"Dyer was determined to get his share of the money from Spencer and cooked up a fake drug deal, allegedly involving a dealer by the name of John Fry. The Fry deal would lure Spencer to the Rifle Club where Dyer could get the money he felt he was owed. Joe Dyer had put his revenge strategy in motion.

"On October 17, 1974, Dyer, Grimes, and Logan met Spencer and Cannon at the Rifle Club. Steve Cannon, for all practical purposes, was just along for the ride. Sadly, it's a clear case of being in the wrong place at the wrong time.

"At the Club, Dyer played out the drug-deal charade. After waiting almost an hour, Spencer told the others he'd waited long enough and he and Cannon were leaving. They started walking to his car. It was at this point that Dyer and Grimes shot down Spencer and Cannon in cold blood. Spencer was hit first by a blast from Dyer's shotgun. Joe Dyer knew he had to get the drop on the Vietnam vet; otherwise, Spencer would have used the M1 carbine to defend himself.

"Cannon was shot in the back by Grimes as he attempted to flee the scene. With both young men wounded and lying on the ground, Dyer used his shotgun to make sure the two were dead.

"You have heard from the coroner and longtime law-enforcement officers that these murders were some of the most horrific that they'd ever witnessed.

"Once the smoke cleared, Dyer ordered Grimes and Logan to dig a grave and bury the two young men. Over a thousand dollars was taken from Spencer's body before Dyer stripped the clothes off both men and threw their bodies in the freshly dug hole.

"The next part of his plan was to get rid of Spencer's car. Logan was told to drive the car to Eastgate Shopping Center. Dyer instructed him to leave the car in the parking lot with its windows rolled down and the keys in the ignition. He was hoping it would be stolen. His thinking was that the thieves would be caught and be accused of the murders. But his plan didn't stop there. He had a few other steps to follow.

"Joe Dyer had taken possession of the two dead men's billfolds and had thrown them out on I-24, another tactic to throw off investigators. Lastly, he called the Spencer apartment around ten-thirty and asked to speak to Rick. Of course, he wasn't there, but Dyer thought this would cast out any thought that he had anything to do with the killings.

"Ladies and gentlemen of the jury, Joe Dyer had a devious, well-thought-out plan to kill Spencer and he carried it out to a 'T.' But let's not forget that Donald Chip Grimes was a willing participant."

Next, Assistant DA Lanzo said to the jury, "The defense wants you to think that John Logan fabricated his story. Yes, he was guilty of participating in a burglary at the drugstore and in the robbery and burial of the bodies. But let's not forget that Logan didn't fire a gun out there. His actions at the Rifle Club were directed by Joe Dyer and it was Dyer who masterminded the events that led to the gruesome deaths of those two young men.

"Now let's consider a few more facts about this case. A key witness, John Fry, denied knowing Joe Dyer or having any involvement in a drug deal at the Chattanooga Rifle Club. You'll remember that Dyer earlier testified that Fry was to appear at the Rifle Club on the evening Spencer and Cannon were killed.

"Fry was supposedly going to sell Spencer ten pounds of marijuana that was valued at one thousand dollars. It was this promise by Dyer that lured Spencer to the Rifle Club with money in his pocket to make the buy. As you have already heard, Dyer was angry over the fact that Spencer had lost the stolen pills and wanted revenge.

"Dyer also stated that Carl Logan had been involved in the murders, but we know that wasn't true. Two witnesses placed the younger Logan at his apartment at the time of the killings.

"Mr. Dyer also said that he was not involved in the drugstore break-in. Yet again, another witness testified that Dyer was bragging about the drugstore burglary just days after the event. As you can see, Dyer's comments were out of step with almost every other testimony you have heard during this trial.

"Oh yes, let's not forget that an M1 carbine was found at Dyer's house in a drainpipe. The serial number had been filed off, but we can feel certain it was the one carried by Spencer on the night of his murder. Remember that John Logan testified that Dyer took the M1 as a souvenir.

"Witnesses have testified that Dyer had a history with guns. The proof of this was evident when investigators found an arsenal at his house. Joe Dyer liked to think of himself as a bad dude. He has admitted to frequently carrying a gun with him. Witnesses have stated that he had said, 'No one is going to rip Joe Dyer off.' Remember, several testimonies recounted that Dyer believed that Spencer had ripped him off over the stolen pills from the drugstore."

Lanzo wrapped up the state's closing statement by saying. "Joseph Dyer is a different breed of cat who lives in his inner sanctum with a deadbolt lock on the door. He won't give it a second thought to kill somebody. His motive wasn't so much the money reportedly taken from Spencer, but a demented mind that doesn't want to be ripped off. He was Rick Spencer's and Steve Cannon's executioner.

"As far as Donald Chip Grimes goes, it was a shame he became involved with Dyer. But under the law, Grimes is guilty of aiding and abetting Dyer in the most horrible thing that has happened in this community in a long time. It's a shame that Chip Grimes got messed up with him.

"The defense will most likely point out that John Logan was not a creditable witness, but the reality is Logan's testimony was consistent and in line with the testimonies of other witnesses.

"We believe the testimonies you have heard and the evidence you have seen will make it clear to you to find Joseph Dyer and Donald Grimes guilty of first-degree murder. In the state of Tennessee, a conviction of first-degree murder carries a mandatory death-penalty sentence. Thank you for your service and commitment to finding out the truth. The State rests its case."

The Defense Addresses the Jury

Next the defense addressed the jury. It was Dyer's and Grimes's attorneys Jerry Summers's and Bill Ortwein's turn to make a compelling argument that their clients were innocent of the murder and robbery charges.

Summers started by saying, "The most important issue in this case is the credibility of the state's key witness, John Logan. He is the real heart of the case.

"The state has presented a fantasy through John Logan, who was a well-coached witness. He was willing to help them out to save himself from the death penalty. He's agreed to plead guilty to lesser charges and testify on behalf of the prosecution. In our judgment, the prosecutors made the wrong deal.

"My client, Joe Dyer, testified on Saturday that John Logan killed the victims with the aid of his brother, Carl Logan. Let's face it. The younger Logan was an uncharged accomplice who made the sweetest deal, because he's avoided prosecution altogether."

Summers then brought out the fact that no shotgun, the murder weapon, had been found. He also talked about the M1 carbine that was discovered at Joe Dyer's house and pointed out that there was no concrete proof that linked it to Mr. Spencer. He went on to say, "The state only has Logan's testimony who said Dyer took the M1 for a souvenir.

"I also want to point out the testimony of John Fry. The state brought him down here from Kentucky to tell you he didn't know Joseph Dyer and had nothing to do with the drug deal planned at the Rifle Club. Do you want to take the word of a convict and a drug addict? I don't know how you could believe a word the man had to say."

Then he finished his argument. "The only thing the state has provided is a bunch of hearsay statements. They have no real physical evidence against my client. Their case is built around the testimonies of a bunch of liars. Joe Dyer is innocent and you've heard his story."

Dyer's attorney returned to his seat at the defense table and it was Bill Ortwein's turn to address the jury. Up to this point in the trial, Grimes's attorney had been fairly quiet. Grimes had elected not to testify and his lawyer's strategy was to let Summers take the lead in the case. During cross-examination, Ortwein had asked only a few questions here and there of a few of the witnesses.

Ortwein also hammered on Logan's credibility.

"John Logan has given the police three different statements. On November 27, 1974, he denied involvement with the murders. Then two days later, he told investigators about the murders, but didn't mention Donald Grimes' involvement. Once he's indicted, he comes up with yet a third version of the events that happened in October.

"The third edition of Logan's statement mentioned my client. It was the first time Donald Grimes was mentioned to the authorities. Logan implied that Donald Grimes shot Cannon in the back with a forty-five-caliber pistol. He said this only after he'd learned that a bullet had been discovered in Cannon's body and became afraid he might be charged with firing it. As you can see, Logan's story changes as he feels he needs to, in order to save his own skin."

Ortwein continued to attack Logan's credibility. He finished his comments by saying, "Ladies and gentlemen of the jury, little evidence has been brought out against my client concerning his involvement with the Chattanooga Rifle Club murders. We trust you'll find Donald Grimes innocent of the charges against him. Thank you!"

As Ortwein returned to his seat next to Chip Grimes, Jerry Summers rose from his chair and walked back to the jury box. Before saying a word, Summers looked at each member of the jury. Then he broke the silence. "The biggest crime Joe Dyer is guilty of is making the mistake of trying to help John and Carl Logan. He's also tarnished a good family name by getting involved with people associated with drugs.

"Mr. Ortwein has pointed out that John Logan can't be trusted, because his story changes to fit his needs. Logan has made a deal with the state. He'll serve a few weeks in the workhouse, then start smoking a little pot and let his hair grow out.

"There is nothing to link Dyer to the murders other than Logan's testimony. The fact of the matter is that it was Joe Dyer's word against John Logan's. We've outlined how his word changes as the wind blows. We trust you will find Joe Dyer innocent."

The State's Final Response

The state was allowed to give a final rebuttal to the defense's closing arguments.

Lanzo started by saying, "Mr. Summers is correct; no shotgun was found and an M1 carbine was found in a drainpipe at the Dyers house. Law enforcement has searched the entire county for the shotgun and had no luck. My guess is that it's at the bottom of Chickamauga Lake. But even without the shotgun, we know a shotgun was used to kill Spencer and Cannon and we know Dyer fired the shots.

"Concerning the M1, the serial number had been filed off and there is no way to positively trace it back to Rick Spencer. But isn't it a little odd that an M1 would be stashed in a drainpipe, when thirty feet away in the basement was virtually a weapon museum? If it was just a gun, it would have been in the basement with the rest of the collection. Clearly, Dyer took it from Spencer as a trophy and hid it when the police were on his tail.

"Mr. Summers has also tried to discredit John Fry's testimony by saying he was a drug addict. There is no doubt that he did have a drug problem, but according to the witness from Moccasin Bend, Fry is now clean. Let's face it, even a drug addict knows if he knows someone or not and John Fry doesn't know Joe Dyer. Dyer made up the whole John Fry-selling-pot story to get Rick Spencer to the Rifle Club, so he could murder him.

"Now, concerning Mr. Grimes, his involvement began with the drugstore break-in. He was also a willing accomplice to this heinous crime and if he didn't shoot Cannon in the back, the young man might have gotten away.

"Rick Spencer was a Vietnam veteran and had served his country. He survived the war only to be gunned down in an ambush orchestrated by Joe Dyer. There was no doubt that Spencer was dealing drugs and was guilty of that, but he didn't deserve to die.

"Not only were they brutally killed, Spencer and Cannon were stripped of their clothes and their dignity, then thrown in a hole. Dyer and Grimes tried not to say anything and tried not to get caught, but thanks to Spencer's friends, the evidence always came back to the trigger men, Joe Dyer and Chip Grimes.

"The killing of Spencer and Cannon was the most crazed, most vicious, and most horrible crime that has happened in our community in a long time. The defense has tried to discredit John Logan's testimony, while Dyer's version of the slayings was just unbelievable."

The prosecutor was quiet for a moment or two as he slowly paced back and forth in front of the jury box. Then he said, "Ladies and gentlemen of the jury, the truth is Joe Dyer and Donald Grimes killed Rick Spencer for a thousand dollars and they killed Steve Cannon merely because he was a friend of Spencer's."

There was a long pause, then Lanzo said, "There is no punishment fitting for what the defendants did. Once again, we are asking you, the people of the jury, to find Joseph Dyer and Donald Grimes guilty of first-degree murder and grand larceny. We are confident you will make the proper decision. Thank you!"

Stan Lanzo returned to his seat next to Dave Rotroff. The two men shook hands. Their job was over. It was now up to the jury to see if they agreed with the state.

Chapter 9—Decision Time

After the closing statements from both sides, Judge DiRisio turned the case over to the jury. The courtroom was adjourned.

As the bailiff led the jurors back to the jury room, a group of spectators headed over to the Brass Register for cocktails and something to eat. Once they were settled around the bar, the Rifle Club murder-trial debate began. A variety of topics were discussed, including the recent witnesses, the judge's demeanor, the analysis of each juror, the attorneys, and of course the defendants.

The conversation eventually moved to Logan versus Dyer. The question seemed to be, whose story was believable? The overwhelming majority felt Logan was telling the truth. After all, Logan looked believable, he showed emotion, and came across as being remorseful. A few pointed out that there were just too many inconsistencies with Dyer's story, whereas Logan's testimony lined up with most of the others that testified. One young lady made the comment that Dyer just looked guilty, with his dark eyes and black-rimmed glasses, and was unemotional during the entire trial. Some readily agreed.

The Dyer and Logan conversations eventually shifted over to Grimes. Most of the members of the barroom jury felt his actions, or lack thereof, were strange for a man facing the electric chair. He'd shown little emotion and hadn't said a word during the entire trial. Someone said, "I thought he would have been a key part of the defense's strategy. His testimony could have supported Dyer's story and helped to discredit Logan."

As they continued the debate, a few were also puzzled why Logan hadn't mentioned Grimes during his initial confession to the TBI agent. Apparently, it was only after Logan had been indicted and was in jail that he talked about Grimes.

Someone said, "Yeah, it looks like it was Logan's amended statement that got Grimes called before the grand jury and indicted. I wonder why Logan didn't mention him at first?"

Another replied, "I have no idea."

Then, during Dyer's version of what happened, he stated that Grimes was just along for the ride and had no part in the planning or the shooting. A patron spoke up and said, "It's almost like Dyer was trying to protect him for some reason or another, but why?"

No one had that answer.

Someone speculated, "Maybe it had something to do with Grimes' legal problems in Alabama. Maybe Dyer was involved in that and Grimes covered for him, so Dyer owed him."

"That's possible. After all, it seemed like Dyer didn't mind sharing the stolen cashier's checks with Grimes, but killed Spencer for the money that was allegedly owed. But let's face it. We just don't know anything about Grimes's Alabama problems."

As the talks around the bar went on, there was little doubt that Grimes was involved. After all, he was part of the gang. He participated in the drugstore break-in, he was in the car at Spencer's apartment when it was announced that the proposed drug deal was on, and he was at the Rifle Club the night of the murders. Most believed Grimes was guilty, but no one knew why he hadn't defended himself during the trial.

"He looked like he's already accepted his fate, but why? I'm not sure we're going to find out."

The bar crowd finally dispersed, and most would be back in the courtroom the next day to see what the jury had to say.

The Jury Convenes

While some were having a good time at the Brass Register, the jurors were settling in the jury room to spend their evening making life-or-death decisions. The room was fairly large. In the middle was a large rectangular oak table. On it sat two large pitchers of ice water, along with 16 or so glasses. There were 16 wooden chairs around the table, with one at each end and seven on each side.

One side of the room was lined with wooden bookcases that stood from floor to ceiling. They were full of brownish-colored case-law reference books. On the opposite side of the room were large windows covered with white venetian blinds. There was a serving table against one wall. Where there was no furniture or windows, extra chairs were randomly placed against the walls.

After a short bathroom break, Judge DiRisio met with the group and gave them their instructions. He reviewed with them their duties and responsibilities as jurors. Then the judge explained that their job was to determine if Dyer and Grimes were guilty of grand larceny and first-degree murder. He noted that these were two different charges and a vote must be taken on each count.

The judge went on to explain that in the state of Tennessee, death by electrocution was the mandatory penalty for a first-degree murder conviction. First-degree murder had to be premeditated and deliberate. Next, he told them that they had to be unanimous in their decision in order to convict the defendants of the charges. A few jurors had questions, which the judge answered.

Then he said, "There's one more thing. If you find the defendants guilty of first-degree murder, you must recommend death by electrocution. It's the law." The judge left the room.

As the jury room door closed, the members of jury sat in silence as they tried to absorb what Judge DiRisio had just said. The jury was made up of eight men and four women, six black and six white. The 12 knew that they would be faced with one of the toughest tasks of their lives and they knew that the lives of two men hung in the balance of their decision.

The silence was broken when one of the jurors said, "Well, let's get started and elect a foreman."

The foreman is the leader and facilitator of the jury. It's his or her job to keep the others on task and be the contact with the judge in the event of questions or problems. Following a brief discussion, the jurors selected a middle-aged man as the foreman and the discussion began.

After an hour and a half of discussion, the jurors had reached a stalemate on the murder charge. One of the jurors refused to agree to the murder charge because of the mandatory death penalty. At this impasse, the foreman contacted the judge. Judge DiRisio suggested they start by trying to reach a decision on the lesser charge, then come back to the murder charge. He instructed them to continue talking until they had a decision.

The jury took a short break, then returned to the room. The foreman took the judge's advice and told the group to start with the armed robbery of Spencer and Cannon. In less than 30 minutes, the men and women of the jury voted unanimously. Dyer and Grimes were found guilty of the larceny charge.

With the robbery charge settled, it was back to the murder discussion. It continued to be a lengthy debate. As the clock ticked past midnight, a haze of cigarette smoke clung to the ceiling of the jury room. The table was cluttered with an assortment of glassware. Several large, thick, emerald-green, glass ashtrays full of ashes and cigarette butts sat randomly around the sturdy wooden table, interspersed with empty Coke bottles, partly filled water glasses, and half-full white ceramic cups of coffee. White plates with food scraps or half-eaten sandwiches virtually covered the remaining space on the big table. There was hardly any room left for the yellow legal pads of paper each juror had for note taking.

When the clock struck one a.m., there was still no unanimous agreement on the murder charge and the jurors were spent. At this point, the foreman announced a recess and the group retired for the night. They would resume the next morning around 8:30.

The Verdict

When the jurors returned to the room the next morning, the tabletop was clear, except for two pitchers of water and drinking glasses. By 8:45 on December 16, the jurors had settled down in their chairs to full coffee cups and lit cigarettes. The fate of Dyer and Grimes was still in question. At nine a.m., the courtroom was about half-full and by 10, all the seats were filled as people anticipated the return at any moment of the jury.

Meanwhile, the debate in the jury room went on. The conversation continued for almost four more hours before the foreman finally notified the judge that they'd reach a verdict.

The attorneys and the defendants were summoned back to the courtroom for the reading of the verdict. At 12:57 p.m., the jurors marched back into the courtroom. The media was jockeying for positions to get the best view of the defendants. Once the jury had been seated in the box, the judge called the court back to order and the foreman handed a piece of paper to Judge DiRisio, on which the jury's decision had been written.

The judge read the note to himself. It said, "The men and women of the jury find Joe Dyer and Donald Grimes guilty of murder in the first degree with a recommendation of mercy."

The judge read it again to himself.

Then he folded up the piece of paper and handed it back to the bailiff. With a look of disappointment over the lack of a penalty, he said to the jury, "Your verdict is incomplete. You must return to the jury room and finalize the verdict."

The bailiff led the 12 weary souls back to the jury room.

The judge ordered a recess until the jury returned with a complete verdict. As the announcement was made, sighs of "Oh's" rang out throughout the courtroom. The defendants, attorneys, gallery, and media would have to wait longer for the final decision.

As the jury was getting seated back in their room, the judge walked in and asked to speak with the foreman. The two men went out in the hall. As the door shut, the remaining jurors looked at one another and wondered what was going on.

In the hallway the judge and the foreman spoke for a few minutes.

When the foreman returned to the jury room, all eyes were on him as he took his place at the head of the long wooden table.

He sipped from his water glass, then said, "I know we're all tired, but we have to define the penalty for the first-degree murder charge. Frankly, the state of Tennessee has assumed the full burden of guilt, because they have assigned the penalty for the charge. Remember, it's the law that a first-degree murder conviction comes with the penalty of death by electrocution. The state determined that, not us. I know some of us don't like the death penalty, but we have to vote on the charges at hand.

"Remember, our job is to determine if the defendants are guilty of murder. If we agree, then they'll be convicted in the first-degree and it must be accompanied with the penalty. I suggest that we vote again and this time we vote for the first-degree murder charge with the death penalty and ask for mercy. I believe if we do this, we've done our job with compassion for human life. Does everyone agree with taking a vote on what I've suggested?"

All agreed and a few minutes later, they all submitted their ballots to the foreman.

He counted them and said, "We are unanimous. Thank you for your hard work. I believe we can leave here being proud of our work and with a clear conscience. I'll notify the judge."

The judge summoned the lawyers and the defendants back to the courtroom.

A few minutes later, at 1:42 p.m., the tired jury filed back into the courtroom. Court was called back in session and once again, the foreman handed the judge a piece of paper with their decision written on it.

Judge DiRisio said, "Would the defendants please rise."

Dyer and Grimes stood along with their attorneys. Then he gave the foreman a nod and asked him to read the verdicts to the court.

The courtroom was completely silent as the foreman began to speak. "On the charges of grand larceny, the jury finds the defendants guilty."

He took a long pause before reciting the next set of charges. He cleared his throat and said in a matter-of-fact tone, "On the charges of murder, we find the defendants guilty of two counts of murder in the first degree and recommend the death penalty as mandated by state law, but ask the court for mercy."

The judge thanked the jurors for their work.

Judge DiRisio then turned to the two defendants who were still standing and said, "On the charge of grand larceny, you are hereby sentenced to ten years in the state penitentiary. On the charge of first-degree murder, you are sentenced to death by electrocution. You will begin serving your time on death row at the Tennessee State Penitentiary in Nashville. You will be held there until you are executed, which has been set for July 21, 1976."

The two men took the decision calmly.

The judge then asked the guilty men if they had anything to say.

Dyer, showing no emotion, looked at the judge and said, "Your Honor, you've convicted two innocent men."

Surprisingly, the packed courtroom remained fairly quiet as a low buzz of whispers permeated throughout the room.

The defense attorneys, Summers and Ortwein, immediately moved for a mistrial. This was the third mistrial filing of the trial.

Summers argued, "The jury has returned a compromised verdict, evident by their mercy amendment to the punishment. The recommendation implies the jury is under the false impression that it would have some legal impact on their sentencing. In other words, they were not told that the mercy amendment had no bearing on the mandated punishment and my client still got the death penalty."

Judge DiRisio replied, "Your motion is so noted."

He gave the defense attorneys 30 days to file a motion for a new trial and said Dyer and Grimes would be held in the county jail without bond, pending the decision. Even if the mistrial was denied, it was expected that the defense team would appeal the decision.

The judge once again hit his gavel on the bench and announced, "Court is adjourned!"

County sheriff officers handcuffed the guilty men and escorted them back to the jailhouse.

The verdict clearly indicated that the jury believed the state witness John Logan's testimony instead of Dyer's version of the murders on October 17. The weeklong trial had taken its toll on all those who had been involved.

Chapter 10—The Aftermath

As soon as Judge DiRisio struck his gavel to the bench, the rumbling of conversations echoed throughout the courthouse as spectators exited the venue. The biggest trial in Chattanooga in the past 10 years was over and everyone was discussing the outcome. What had started in October 1974 with the disappearance of a Vietnam veteran and a recent high-school graduate had ended 14 months later with the death penalty for two men in their early 20s.

As the courtroom emptied out, Lillie Spencer remained in her seat. She just stared ahead, tears rolling down her cheeks. She used a tissue to absorb the moisture. It was finally over. She remembered that night the nightmare began. She was in France and called home, expecting to talk to Rick, but finding out he was missing.

She snapped out of the trance and, realizing she was the only one left in the courtroom, got up and left. The once-crowded hallways were almost deserted. As she exited the building, she walked by a few reporters who had gathered on the steps comparing notes and looking for interviews. Fortunately for her, they were oblivious to her, and she walked by herself to her parked car.

The news media was trying to finish their stories. They wanted to hear from the lawyers and members of the jury. They were anxious to get comments from the attorneys on both sides. The prosecutors only said they had nothing else to say that hadn't already been said to the jury. On the defense side, even the normally talkative Jerry Summers was short on words, saying only there would be an appeal in the future.

The media was also seeking out jury members in hopes of getting a comment about what had transpired in the jury room. Several members of the jury were in tears as they left the courtroom. All except one refused to comment on what had gone on behind closed doors over the past several days. The sole spokesman's only comment was short, "We're all in a turmoil right now."

The lack of commentary didn't help the storyline very much, but it didn't matter, as the reporters had to get moving in order to meet their deadlines. There was no time to waste. They all kicked into high gear as they hustled to get their reports filed for the next edition or newscast.

One of the local newspaper reporters rushed to one of the phone booths in the courthouse lobby, put a dime in the payphone, and placed a call to the city editor. He wanted to make sure he reserved space in the morning paper for the full story. The other local newspaper reporter rushed back to his office and put the finishing touches on his report of the trial. His story would come out in the afternoon edition.

While the print reporters hurried to make press time, the television reporters set up shop outside the courthouse. The three local news stations, channels 3, 9, and 12, were scattered out around the grounds of the white government building. Each had a camera crew filming their reporter as they recapped the findings of the jury. They were all hurrying to make the 6 o'clock news.

While the news people were trying to make deadlines, the Brass Register patrons headed to the bar for a final review of the day's proceedings and the trial. Once the beers and drinks started flowing, talk about the day intensified. Most weren't surprised by the verdicts, as most of them had already plugged in the electric chair for Dyer and Grimes. There were more comments about how long it took the jury to reach the final verdict.

The excitement of the trial was over and Chattanooga, except those affected by the murders, went back to life as usual. Death-penalty cases are always high stress and become emotional for everyone involved. It had been a particularly hard-fought case on both sides.

The week-long trial had also taken its toll on the jury members. The stress could be seen on their faces, whether they were black, white, male, or female. These seven days would remain with them for the rest of their lives.

It had also been an emotional roller coaster for the families and friends of the young men who were involved. It would be easier for the friends than the families to move on with their lives, yet the events surrounding the trial would be something they would always remember.

As for the families, the memories would be with them from now on, but the battles for some were far from over. The appeals would come first, followed by other legal filings. Some family members would stay involved, while others would move on and try to put it behind them.

The Day After

The headlines in the December 17, 1975, edition of the *Chattanooga Times* read: "Dyer and Grimes Given Two Death Sentences; Jurors Propose Mercy."

The conviction of Dyer and Grimes for first-degree murder marked only the ninth and tenth times that a Hamilton County criminal-court jury had imposed the death penalty since capital punishment had been reinstated in Tennessee in 1974. The good news, if there was any for the two recently convicted men, was that no one had been put to death in the electric chair in the state since 1960. On top of that, the current governor, Ray Blanton, had said on several occasions that he would "never pull the switch."

The third mistrial motion, which had been filed at the conclusion of the trial, was denied and Dyer and Grimes were sent off to death row.

Life for the Convicts

The two convicted men spent Christmas in jail and by the middle of January, Dyer and Grimes were transferred from the Hamilton County jail to the state penitentiary in Nashville. There, they waited on their pending death sentence; however, their time on death row turned out to be short. Fortunately for them, their date with the executioner, set for July 1976, only six months in the future, was cancelled after Tennessee's death-penalty statute was declared unconstitutional by the U.S. Supreme Court. Their sentence was commuted to life imprisonment.

Now that the anxiety of waiting on their death sentence was over, the two convicts had to adjust to the fact that they would most likely spend the rest of their lives in prison. Soon after having their sentences commuted, they were transferred to the Southeast Tennessee State Regional Correctional Facility in Pikeville.

Grimes seemed content to spend the rest of his life behind bars, but not Dyer. Joe had other thoughts. He wanted out and planned to use every legal option available to him to do it.

Joe Dyer in Prison

Joe knew it would be a long road to gain his freedom, but he never gave up on obtaining his goal. He wasn't eligible for parole until he'd served 30 years. To survive, he kept himself busy. He worked in the pharmacy as a lab technician in the plasma center, and as a law clerk.

He took correspondence courses from the Chattanooga State Community College and in 1995 earned an Associate Degree of Science. He also worked as the editor and photographer of the prison newspaper. He was considered a model prisoner and kept pursuing legal ways to get released, filing several appeals concerning his incarceration.

In the '90s, he appeared in front of the Parole Board. It was the first of what turned out to be more than a half-dozen times over the next 20 years. Each time he made an appearance, his release was vehemently opposed by the Cannon family. Finally, after 40 years behind bars, on January 31, 2014, he was granted parole and released from prison to a halfway house in Crossville, Tennessee. As of this writing Joe Dyer is still living in the Volunteer State. Chip Grimes was a different story.

Grimes Serves the Time

Donald "Chip" Grimes had kept a low profile during the 1975 trial and didn't testify in his own defense. He and his defense team relied on Dyer's attorneys to fight their battle. Once in prison, the one-time engineering major seemed resigned to his fate and remained there the rest of his life. He died in prison around 2020.

The difference in Dyer and Grimes's prison time was somewhat of a surprise. Based on the testimony given during the 1975 trial, one would have expected that Donald Grimes would get out of prison long before Joe Dyer. This is based on the fact Grimes fired only one shot, as opposed to Dyer's multiple shotgun blasts into Spencer and Cannon. So how did just the opposite happen?

Most likely, it was based on who had the desire to get out of prison. From the time the prison door shut behind him, Joe Dyer was determined to regain his freedom. He developed a plan and sustained the drive and the tenacity to keep fighting for four full decades until he was freed. Grimes, on the other hand, apparently had neither the fight nor the desire and became content with prison life.

While Dyer and Grimes adjusted to life in prison, others involved with the trial wanted to put the events of October 17, 1974, behind them.

The Logans and the Lawyers

John Logan spent some time in the Hamilton County jail, but never had to go to state prison. He remained in Chattanooga and as of this writing, he's still there. His brother Carl started a construction business and ran it successfully until he died from cancer in 2013.

Dave Prickett, one of Rick Spencer's roommates, went on to become a lawyer. He practiced law until his death.

Judge Joseph DiRisio stayed on the bench for many years and passed away in 1997 at the age of 69.

The prosecutors, Stan Lanzo and Dave Rotroff, both continued to practice law in Chattanooga for many years. Lanzo spent over six decades in law, both as a prosecutor and a defense attorney. He became a big supporter of a Christmas celebration for foster children. For many years, he headed gift drives for these children in the city. He wanted to make sure every child received a Christmas present. He succumbed to Parkinson in 2021.

Dave Rotroff spent most of his 50 years of law in the district attorney's office. He retired to North Carolina where he passed away in 2020.

The defense attorneys, Bill Ortwein and Jerry Summers, put in long years of service as attorneys. Ortwein continued to work as a defense attorney. He also served two terms as a state senator. He died in 2019.

As of this writing, Jerry Summers is still practicing law as a defense attorney. He has also become a writer. His articles regularly appear on the local e-news site: Chattanoogan.com. He has also written several books. Summers has become one of the city's unofficial historians concerning sports, politics, and 20th-century stories.

The Logans and the legal professionals all moved on from the Rifle Club murders case. Rick Spencer's mother tried to do the same.

Lillie Spencer

Eight days after Joe Dyer and Donald Grimes were convicted, Lillie Spencer once again attended the Christmas Eve service at Central Baptist Church of Woodmore. It was the second Christmas Eve service she attended without her beloved son Rick.

As she sat in the pew, she remembered how happy she'd been three years earlier sitting in the same place next to her son. Rick had just been discharged from the Army and was home. Her prayers had been answered as he'd returned safely from Vietnam.

Rick was now gone and Lillie would always grieve the loss of her son. During the service, her mind drifted from the spoken word and the music as she replayed her fond memories of Rick and the joy he'd brought to her life. While Joe Dyer had taken Rick away from her, she would always cherish the memories of him.

At the same time, she was determined to move on with her life. In 1977, she took a new job and moved to Honolulu. She continued working and remarried in 1982. The couple stayed in Hawaii until 1990, then moved to Myrtle Creek, Oregon, a small town in the western-central part of the state. She died out west in 1997, but her body was returned to Tennessee, where she was buried next to Rick at Lakewood Memorial Gardens. They were once again together.

Until the day that she died, she knew that Rick wasn't the same man he was before he left for Vietnam. The war had changed him, and the change had cost him his life.

Epilogue

Jerry Summers said it best during the trial, "What a waste of youth." The statement certainly applied to the five young men involved in what transpired that night on October 17, 1974.

Joe Dyer and Chip Grimes were smart guys and had promising futures ahead of them.

John Logan had many opportunities before him, based on his wrestling accomplishments, but he never fulfilled his potential. In addition, he was haunted by the memories of the Rifle Club for the rest of his life.

Steve Cannon came from a good family, but never got the chance to prove himself.

Rick Spencer had a great work ethic and an entrepreneurial spirit. There's no telling what he could have become.

All five had tremendous potential with their lives in front of them, but they never came to fruition, due to drugs. Jerry Summers was right; it was truly a waste of youth!

Rick Spencer was at the center of the story. Ironically, the place where my dad and I had taken him to learn how to shoot guns, the Chattanooga Rifle Club, was the last place he would see on Earth. Rick was like a lot of men who went to Vietnam. He volunteered to serve his country, but came back a changed man. War does that to everyone who experiences it, especially those who fight. The horror of battle, the loneliness of being away from home, and the stress of not knowing what tomorrow will bring are all part of military conflicts.

The Vietnam War was different than all other wars in which American soldiers had fought. It was directed by the politicians and had a flawed strategy. The country was involved in Vietnam for almost 20 years, but from the start, the Americans had no real chance of winning.

The results of the war certainly had nothing to do with the American soldiers. They fought as hard as any before or after, but despite their efforts, victory was unattainable. In addition, what started out as an effort to contain communism evolved into a conflict within the United States that divided the nation, and the soldiers were caught in the figurative crossfire.

Returning Vietnam veterans were disrespected by the country they served and it has taken many years for them to be appreciated. Today, these vets frequently hear, "Thank you for your service." In 1982, the Vietnam Veterans Memorial was completed in Washington, D.C. It was built to honor those who died or went missing during the war.

Since Vietnam, American armies have been involved in several other wars. Some we've committed to winning, while others we've committed to just being there. Hopefully, next time we commit to sending American forces into battle, we will be committed to winning.

But regardless of what the politicians do, let's keep one thing always in mind. We must respect the servicemen and women who are serving our country. After all, they are just following orders.

Rick Spencer survived Vietnam, only to return home where, not too soon thereafter, he lost his life. Was Vietnam the cause of his death? Not necessarily, but the war did change him, and that change contributed to his fate. Although his name isn't found on the Vietnam Veterans Memorial Wall, because he wasn't killed in battle, he can certainly be considered a casualty of war.

As for now, the name R.C. (Rick) Spencer can be found on the inside wall of the mausoleum at Lakewood Memorial Gardens East in Chattanooga, Tennessee.

Sources

Ancestry
How Life Out of Prison Can Be Harder than Life in Prison
Lakewood Memory Gardens
Tennessee Department of Corrections
The *Chattanooga News-Free Press*
The *Chattanooga Times*
The Rattler/Firebird Association
Wikipedia

About the Author

Where's Rick? is Buck Buchanan's fourth published book.

His third book, *Behind the Walls,* tells the story of the industry of which he was a part for over 35 years. The business started from scratch and became a $3 billion industry.

Buck's second title, *The Game of Sales,* is a business book based on his experience as a sales manager.

His first book was released in the fall of 2015. *First and Thirty* is centered on a high-school football team in the south during the 1970 season. It follows the lives of the football players and their friends as they undergo the trials and tribulations of being in high school during the tumultuous years of the Vietnam War and social unrest.

Buck Buchanan was born in Chattanooga, Tennessee. He graduated from Chattanooga High School and in 1976 received a BS degree in Business Administration from the University of Tennessee at Chattanooga. After graduation, he moved to Atlanta and began a business career that spanned 40 years, including 10 in California managing a large business unit. He now lives in Marietta, Georgia.

Buck is married to Cindy, his high-school sweetheart, and they have three children and five grandchildren.

www.ingramcontent.com/pod-product-compliance
Lightning Source LLC
Chambersburg PA
CBHW051428090426
42737CB00014B/2867